101 Activities for *Delivering Knock Your Socks Off Service*

101 Activities for
Delivering Knock Your Socks Off Service

Performance Research Associates
Ann Thomas and Jill Applegate

AMACOM

AMERICAN MANAGEMENT ASSOCIATION

New York • Atlanta • Brussels • Chicago • Mexico City • San Francisco
Shanghai • Tokyo • Toronto • Washington, D. C.

Special discounts on bulk quantities of AMACOM books are available to corporations, professional associations, and other organizations. For details, contact Special Sales Department, AMACOM, a division of American Management Association, 1601 Broadway, New York, NY 10019.

Tel.: 212-903-8316. Fax: 212-903-8083.

E-Mail: specialsls@amanet.org

Website: www.amacombooks.org/go/specialsales

To view all AMACOM titles, go to: www.amacombooks.org

This publication is designed to provide accurate and authoritative information in regard to the subject matter covered. It is sold with the understanding that the publisher is not engaged in rendering legal, accounting, or other professional service. If legal advice or other expert assistance is required, the services of a competent professional person should be sought.

Library of Congress Cataloging-n-Publication

Thomas, Ann
101 activities for delivering knock your socks off service / Ann Thomas and Jill Applegate.
     p. cm
Includes bibliographical references and index.
ISBN-13: 978-0-8144-1444-6
ISBN-10: 0-8144-444-3
1. Customer service. 2. Customer relations—Management. I. Applegate, Jill. II. Title.
III. One hundred one activities for delivering knock your socks off service.

HF5415.5.T477   2009
658.8'12—dc22   2008053482

Art work © 2009 John Bush.

Printing Number
10 9 8 7 6 5 4 3 2 1

CONTENTS

SECTION TWO
The How-To's of *Knock Your Socks Off Service*

SECTION FIVE
Knock Your Socks Off Fitness

OUR THANKS

As with any book, its creation cannot be ascribed solely to its authors; many people played a role in its completion.

This book came about because of you! So many of our clients and seminar participants kept asking us, "Can you give us more?" "How can we follow up on this seminar on a weekly basis?" "We need to reinforce this training—what can we do?" and on and on. You would no longer be denied! So, a special thank-you goes to each and every seminar and workshop attendee who demanded this book be written!

Editor extraordinaire, Dave Zielinski, once again exceeded expectations with his careful attention to the *Knock Your Socks Off* flavor and styling. Thanks, Dave—we can't imagine doing one of these without you!

We are so pleased to once again include illustrations from the late John Bush. John left us way too soon in 2006, but we could not have a *Socks Off* book without him. We spent hours going through the art that John so carefully created for the previous books, and were blown away once again by his engaging wit and his unique ability to capture exactly what we were looking for. This book includes the "Best Of" John's work, and we are grateful to Nancy Bush for generously allowing us to reprint them.

Ellen Kadin has been our editor with AMACOM for many years. It's comforting to know she's just a phone call or an e-mail away. We value her role and expertise—and she coordinates a fabulous AMACOM team.

A very special thank-you to Susan Zemke, whose enthusiasm and excitement for this book is so appreciated. We are grateful to Susan for her constant support and commitment to keeping Ron's legacy at the fore.

Ann thanks her husband, Jim, for his patience, and her girls for their "You go, Mom!" enthusiasm. She'd also like to thank her co-author for all the little "pushes" along the way to make our deadlines.

Jill thanks her family for their love and continual support throughout this process and all her endeavors. She'd also like to give a special shout out to Russ Rolinger, who gave her her first foray in customer service by hiring her as a high school waitress many years ago!

None of this would be possible without the groundbreaking work started by Ron Zemke in 1985. Ron's efforts in the world of service quality are near legendary. And we are honored to be a small part in continuing his efforts.

Ann Thomas
Jill Applegate
Performance Research Associates
January 2009

INTRODUCTION

ABOUT THIS BOOK

Over the years, as we've worked with thousands of customer-service professionals around the world, we have heard a common request. As people have read the book *Delivering Knock Your Socks Off Service*, or attended a workshop based on its concepts, they've wondered if any follow-up training activities existed that they could use with their service teams. What these customer-service leaders sought were short, impactful learning exercises to help build on or reinforce ideas found in the book or discussed in our workshops.

We realized we would be remiss if we didn't listen closely to our customers and try to meet their needs. Indeed, it would be tantamount to not walking our service talk. That is a big reason this book now rests in your hands. We hope, in fact, not to have simply met your needs with this collection of *Knock Your Socks Off* training exercises but to have exceeded your expectations.

While the 101 activities included here serve as natural companion pieces to the book and workshops, they also are designed to be used in stand-alone fashion. Any customer-service team in virtually any industry can benefit from the exercises without prior exposure to the *Knock Your Socks Off Service* line of products.

We created the activities with the demands of the busy customer-service function in mind. Whether you're serving customers in a vast call center, on the floor of a retail organization, or at the window of a financial institution, your plate runneth over with customer questions, problems, new products or services, or new technologies. We know there are days when you are fielding these questions, troubleshooting the problems, learning about the new products, or mastering the new technologies, and you barely have time to come up for air.

That's why most of the activities in the book can be completed in 30 minutes or less. They are designed to be used as motivational sessions before your team starts its work shift, as part of brown-bag lunch seminars, during regular teambuilding sessions, or as short add-ons to existing customer-service training sessions. The activities will help you sustain your competitive service edge without the significant expense of additional training or seminars.

The exercises come in a variety of formats and lengths, from brainstorming to role-plays to games to secret shopping trips. But underlying all is a common theme: an activity grounded in adult learning principles that stress learning by doing, have a focus on real-world customer-service challenges, and ease the transfer of training back to the workplace. We believe adults learn best when they are fully engaged and participative, and when training is based not only on the instructor's or manager's expertise but also on the hard-won lessons and insights shared by frontline service professionals. Customer service is at once both one of the most demanding and one of the most rewarding jobs on the globe. It can make clear the difference between organizations that succeed and organizations that struggle, because the latter haven't yet learned one of the paramount rules of customer service: *When customers truly feel you have their best interests at heart, they'll stick to your organization like Velcro®.*

What you do is vital to your organization—now more than ever before. We hope you use these activities to continue building and honing the customer-service skills and attitudes that give your organization that all-important service edge—and that you share with your team a lot of fun and laughs in the process.

The Fundamentals of
Knock Your Socks Off Service

The phrase *"Knock Your Socks Off Service"* often conjures up feats of service daring-do, of the above-and-beyond acts of customer service that leave jaws agape, eyes wide, and big smiles on clients' faces. Our minds fix on the service worker who drives desperately through the night to get a critical part to the auto-repair shop, the fast-food manager who personally delivers items missing from a drive-thru order to a customer's place of business, or the call-center agent who moves heaven and earth to fix a problem for an aggrieved customer.

While delivering memorable service can and often does include these near-heroic acts, knocking people's socks off with customer care is more about doing the little things right, day in and day out, that by virtue of their rarity set you apart from competitors. Customers have grown used to indifferent, overly automated, robotic, or just plain rude service. When they do encounter caring and knowledgeable service professionals, it's enough to make them walk away in amazement, and to breathlessly tell family, co-workers, or their Internet buddies: "I actually talked to a live customer service person today who seemed to have my best interests at heart."

Delivering *Knock Your Socks Off Service* is, first and foremost, about mastering the fundamentals of service quality. It's about doing what you say you're going to do, and living up to promises you make to customers. It's about being empathetic when customers experience frustrating problems—and taking ownership to fix them, not passing the buck; it's the level of care you'd want if you were in the same boat. It's about knowing your product or service features backward and forward—and how you stack up against the competition—so customers who've researched your offerings on the Web can't stump you with questions or blindside you with independent studies.

Mastering these building blocks of *Knock Your Socks Off Service* begins with understanding what good service is in the minds of customers, a notion that can vary greatly with the individual. While one person might want his customer care brisk and efficient, another might seek more hand-holding, small talk, and detailed explanations. The process continues with becoming proficient in the five all-important RATER factors of service quality: Reliability, Assurance, Tangibles, Empathy, and Responsiveness. To provide the kind of service that keeps finicky customers glued to your organization, you have to keep your promises, provide knowledgeable service, ensure you and your organization "look the part," demonstrate appropriate empathy for customers' problems, and deliver service in a timely fashion.

It is this tapestry of fundamentals, consistently performed, that elevates your company above the faceless service providers hiding behind a voice-mail system; it transforms your company into an organization that keeps customers coming back for more of that increasingly scarce quality in today's business world: competent, high-touch service that sends customers the message that they aren't a nuisance but, rather, the lifeblood of the company.

The activities in this section will help you and your team practice and refine the fundamental skills of service quality, using interactive and engaging learning formats that impart the most knowledge in the shortest amount of time.

Learn, laugh, and enjoy!

ACTIVITY 1

What Customers Want, What Customers Expect

We think we know how our company is perceived—but do we *really?* Our perceptions are formed from the inside looking out. But the most important perspective is that of the external customer. After all, it's how they think and feel, and where they choose to spend their hard-earned dollars, that ultimately determines the fate of our company.

PURPOSE:

✓ To compare and contrast the participants' perceptions against the customer's perceptions

✓ To articulate customer expectations

TIME: 20–30 minutes

DIRECTIONS:

1. Depending on the size of the total group, break into smaller subgroups. The ideal size is 3 to 5 people in each group. Distribute Part A to participants

2. Ask participants to respond to the following question in a large group discussion: Who/what is the mission of our company?

3. After hearing from all groups, ask what similarities or differences they observe among the responses.

4. Ask participants to respond to the next question: What do customers want/expect from our company? Be sure to emphasize that they should strive to see the company through the eyes of the external customer, using their own experience as customers as a guide.

5. After hearing from all groups, ask what similarities or differences they observe among the responses. In addition, ask how the responses were different when taking the customer's perspective.

6. The next "layer" question may be asked: What do customers want or expect from our department? Again, this should be discussed in small groups first.

7. After hearing from all groups, ask how these responses support what customers expect from our company.

8. The next question for thinking and discussion should be answered by each individual: What does the customer expect from me?

9. As you hear from each individual, chart responses. If a response is exactly alike, or very similar to a previous answer, put a check mark (✓) in front of the response to indicate how many times you've heard it.

10. The final discussion should be completed by the entire group. After a quick summary of what you have learned by responding to each question, ask the following: What can we, as a group, do to better meet our customers' expectations?

11. You will now have an action plan to change or improve the service you provide to customers. Distribute Part B, and have each participant write their own action plan.

Look out customer—I'm gonna knock your socks off!

PART A

1. What is the principal mission of our company?

    _____

    _____

    _____

2. What do customers want/expect from our company?

    _____

    _____

    _____

3. What do customers want/expect from our department?

    _____

    _____

    _____

4. What does the customer expect from me?

    _____

    _____

    _____

5. What can we as a group do to better meet our customers' expectations?

    _____

    _____

    _____

PART B

Based on the information you provided in Part A, create an individual action plan that will help you change or improve the service you provide to customers.

1. Name three things you can change *right now* that will improve the level of service you personally provide to customers.

    • _____

      _____

    • _____

      _____

    • _____

      _____

2. Name three things you can change in the next *six months* that will improve the level of service you provide to your customers.

    • _____

      _____

    • _____

      _____

    • _____

      _____

ACTIVITY 2

Who's Your Customer?

Everyone has a customer! As Jan Carlson of Scandinavian Airline Systems once said, "If you're not serving the customer, you'd better be serving someone who is." The people who depend on you inside the organization are just as important as those you serve outside the organization.

PURPOSE:

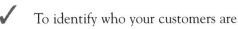 To identify who your customers are

✓ To identify where your customers are

✓ To discover how your work impacts their work and ultimately the customer's satisfaction

TIME: 20 minutes

DIRECTIONS:

1. Ask participants to think about who your customers are, or to whom you need to provide service, by answering these questions:
   - Where does your work go?
   - To whom is your work important?

2. Now, ask participants to list their external and/or internal customers in Activity 2.
   - *External customers* are the people who buy your organization's products and services. They are outside of your own company.

- *Internal customers* work for your organization. They may be at a location in another country, or they may be sitting in the cubicle next to you. Internal customers are people who depend on you and your work in order to complete their work—in order to serve their customers. For example, the internal customers of those taking product orders in customer call centers may be warehouse employees, who rely on service reps' accurate order taking to ship the right goods on time.

Provide participants with examples of internal and external customers.

3. Ask participants to make notes on the two questions at the end of the activity.

4. Use the following questions to debrief after this activity:

- What insights did you gain?

- How differently do we treat internal and external customers?

- What might you add, change, or eliminate in the work that you do?

Identifying Internal and External Customers

   1. My customers are:

External Customers	Internal Customers

   2. Answer the following questions:

     • How does the work you do impact your internal customers' ability to do their own jobs well?

       _____

       _____

       _____

       _____

     • How does your work affect the perception and ultimate satisfaction of external customers?

       _____

       _____

       _____

       _____

ACTIVITY **3**

Knock Your Socks Off Service

Delivering *Knock Your Socks Off Service*—the kind of service that makes a positive, lasting impression on customers—takes more than simple courtesy. Much more! It begins with understanding what good service is, from your customers' point of view. It means exceeding expectations and satisfying the needs of a diverse customer base, including those who might differ from you by culture, age, race, or gender. Above all, it means looking for ways to Wow! and delight your customers in unique and unexpected ways.

PURPOSE:

✓ To articulate what *Knock Your Socks Off Service* means to your group

✓ To incorporate these ideas into your service actions

TIME: 20 minutes

DIRECTIONS:

1. Introduce the concept of service training: why you are doing this, why it's important, what the commitment from the company is to this effort.

2. Ask participants to think of a time when they experienced extraordinary service. What impact did this have on them? Chances are they told many others about it. Have them take a minute or two to jot down some behaviors demonstrated by the service provider or descriptors of the experience.

3. Ask participants to share their lists. Capture these on chart paper or a large white board.

4. When participants hear the words *"Knock Your Socks Off Service,"* ask them what comes to mind—what the phrase means. Cross-reference their words with the words you just captured.

5. Review the bullets listed for Activity 3. Ask participants if they feel they can live up to these expectations on a daily basis. This assumes you will provide training, resources, and ongoing support for the effort! Ask participants to sign the commitment in Activity 3.

Knock Your Socks Off Service **means that you:**

- Take the customer's point of view.

- Understand and exceed customer expectations.

- Satisfy customers' needs.

- Create a positive, memorable experience for customers.

- Are easy to do business with.

- Make a positive, lasting impression on customers.

I, _____, commit to "knock the socks off" all of my customers, internal and external, on a daily basis.

Signed_____   Date_____

ACTIVITY 4

Customers' Ever-Changing Needs

Knock Your Socks Off Service is paying attention to what's important in your customers' eyes. Do you know what counts for your customers? Is it speed of product delivery, technical knowledge, or personable service? What your customers want and need changes constantly. How can you possibly keep up? Let the questions in the next activity guide your personal service efforts.

PURPOSE:

✓ To identify how customer needs change over time

✓ To challenge conventional thinking and practices to anticipate future needs

✓ To build a plan for recognizing changes in customers' needs and implementing suggestions to meet those needs

TIME: 20 minutes

DIRECTIONS:

1. Ask the questions in Activity 4 of either individuals or small groups for their discussion.

2. Have all groups or individuals present their responses. Track ideas for everyone to see.

3. Discuss the changes associates have observed in customer needs and expectations since they began working at the company.

4. Discuss the suggestions associates offer to better anticipate changing customer needs.

5. Develop a plan to implement some of those suggestions. Focus first on the "low-hanging fruit," or the easiest or least expensive changes, you might implement.

Customers' Ever-Changing Needs

1. What do my customers want from me/my company? (Think both about what your customers *need*—those things that create a minimum level of satisfaction—and what your customers *expect*.)

   _____

   _____

2. How have these needs or expectations changed over the last year?

   _____

   _____

3. What additional changes in customer expectations do I anticipate in the future?

   _____

   _____

4. Given the anticipated changes, what suggestions can I offer so that different areas of the company work in harmony for the benefit of my customers?

   _____

   _____

5. What are the details—the little things—that make a big difference in my customers' perceptions of service?

   _____

   _____

ACTIVITY 5

The RATER Factors

One of the cornerstones of *Knock Your Socks Off Service* is what we call the five RATER factors—Reliability, Assurance, Tangibles, Empathy, and Responsiveness. Research by Dr. Leonard Berry, Texas A&M University, shows that customers use these factors with each interaction and they also use them in deciding whether to keep doing business with you. It's critical that all participants consider how they perform in these five essential categories.

PURPOSE:

✓ To personalize the RATER factors to correspond with work participants perform each day

✓ To learn through examples the value of the RATER factors in the work participants do

TIME: 30 minutes

DIRECTIONS:

1. If the RATER factors have not yet been presented, begin with that. If the RATER factors have been presented, a simple review will suffice. (See *Delivering Knock Your Socks Off Service*, 4th edition, Section 1.)

2. Distribute copies of Activity 5 among the participants.

3. Ask participants to describe how each RATER factor is demonstrated through the individual work s/he performs. A good way to set this up

is to say, "If I were the customer, how would I experience you demonstrating Reliability, Assurance, Tangibles, Empathy, and Responsiveness?"

4. Allow 5 to 7 minutes for completion of the writing portion.

5. Debrief participants by asking for examples of each factor, one at a time. Be sure that the examples are specific and relevant. It is not acceptable for participants to use the words in the definitions of each factor in their example. (For example, for Reliability, it's not okay to say, "I provide reports dependably and accurately." It is okay to say, "I promised I would get the customer an answer by 3 PM, and I delivered.")

6. If there is a doubt about the relevance or demonstration of a factor from an example, ask the group to react and respond. Or, if an example is not specific enough, ask the group to provide more details for the example.

7. Ask participants what awareness they have gained from applying the RATER factors to their work.

Primary Application

Identify how to demonstrate each RATER factor based on the work you do.

Think about specific behaviors you could use or activities you could initiate.

- *Reliability:* The customer will know that I am reliable when I _____

_____

_____.

- *Assurance:* The customer will be assured that I am courteous and competent when I _____

_____

_____.

- *Tangibles:* The customer will see tangible evidence of my commitment to service quality when I _____

  _____

  _____.

- *Empathy:* The customer will know that I am empathetic when I _____

  _____

  _____.

- *Responsiveness:* The customer will know that I am responsive when I ___

  _____

  _____.

Alternative Application(s)

1. This same process may be completed at a department or functional level, but should represent a broader application of the factors. (Note: Change the phrase to "The customer will experience my work group as _____ when... .")

2. The exercise also may be done from the perspective of either internal or external customers. Simply clarify that difference when setting up the activity.

ACTIVITY **6**

How Do I RATE?

It's important to know where associates stand in relation to the five all-important RATER factors. Customers use these dimensions to determine the overall service quality of your business—and to decide whether to keep doing business with your organization.

PURPOSE:

✓   To assess individual knowledge and performance using the RATER factors

✓   To build a plan for improvement where need is indicated

TIME: 15–20 minutes

DIRECTIONS:

1. Ask participants to take the brief self-assessment in Part A of Activity 6.

2. Have participants talk in small groups about their responses and reactions to the assessment.

3. Ask participants individually to spend a couple of minutes answering the questions that follow the assessment—Part B of Activity 6.

4. Solicit from each participant one action s/he will take to improve individual RATER factors.

PART A

1. I know what promises my company makes to customers through its advertising, marketing materials, or other company documents.

   ❏ YES   ❏ NO

2. When I personally make a promise to a customer, I always deliver on that promise.

   ❏ YES   ❏ NO

3. After meeting a customer, I am confident that I have uncovered all implied customer promises or expectations.

   ❏ YES   ❏ NO

4. I demonstrate knowledge and competence needed to build customer confidence through my:

   • Detailed knowledge of the product/service

      ❏ YES   ❏ NO

   • Extensive knowledge of the competition

      ❏ YES   ❏ NO

   • Asking pertinent questions that gets my customer talking about his/her needs

      ❏ YES   ❏ NO

   • Listening carefully and quickly to identify the appropriate match of product/service or alternate provider that will exceed customer needs

      ❏ YES   ❏ NO

5. Everything the customer sees, hears, touches, smells, or tastes is something I would be honored to receive myself.

   ❏ YES   ❏ NO

This activity is available at: www.amacombooks.org/go/101ActDKYSOS
© 2009 AMACOM, a division of American Management Association.

6. My personal appearance is always clean, tasteful, and a step above what people expect.

❏ YES   ❏ NO

7. I make each customer feel important as an individual by being respectful (such as finding out what s/he wants to be called, being sensitive to the customer's time, focusing all my attention on the interaction).

❏ YES   ❏ NO

8. I confidently use a variety of communication styles to match the personality of each customer.

❏ YES   ❏ NO

9. I work with customers to create acceptable and realistic deadlines.

❏ YES   ❏ NO

10. I always follow up with my customer when I say I will whether or not I have the information they need.

❏ YES   ❏ NO

PART B

1. Where do I need to improve?

_____

_____

_____

_____

_____

_____

2. How will I work to make a change?

    _____

    _____

    _____

    _____

    _____

    _____

    _____

3. By when?

    _____

    _____

    _____

    _____

    _____

    _____

    _____

4. What assistance do I need to accomplish this change/improvement?

    _____

    _____

    _____

    _____

    _____

    _____

    _____

The Value of Reliability

Reliability is doing what you promised, dependably and accurately. We make promises every day to both internal and external customers. *Knock Your Socks Off Service* means repeating this effort consistently and predictably. When the customer experiences solid delivery of the promise every time, you are recognized as Reliable!

PURPOSE:

✓   To see the value of consistently delivering what is promised

✓   To build a plan for making promises that participants can deliver

TIME: 20 minutes

DIRECTIONS:

1. Ask participants to think of businesses that, based on their personal experience, consistently deliver a product or service as promised. List the businesses.

2. Ask participants to describe the reasons they continue to do business with these companies. Look for responses like "I can count on them," "I know what I'm going to get," "I feel like the business cares about me," "There are never any surprises."

3. Ask participants to give examples of businesses that are inconsistent in delivering a product or service.

4. Discuss how these latter businesses (#3 above) elicit responses that are different from those of the customers of the former set of companies

(#1 above). Look for responses like, "It depends on who you get to serve you," "I have to work harder to get what I need," "I get a reluctant feeling when I may have to go to that company," "I hear different answers from different people," "It makes me really frustrated," "I tell people to be careful if they do business there," "I won't go back."

5. Ask participants to think about the value of repeat business and how that helps build a relationship between a company and its customers. Look for responses like, "I don't have to think much or work very hard doing business there," "People recognize me when I go there," "I get a favor if I ask," "I don't question the information I get from them," "I am confident the people are knowledgeable."

6. Transfer this type of thinking to your own company and what your customers experience when they do business with you. What can customers consistently count on when they interact with your organization?

7. Ask participants to suggest ways to be more realistic in how they make promises to customers, both internal and external. You might add suggestions like: asking the customer what he or she expects, negotiating a more reasonable time frame for delivery, listening for any sense of urgency in the customer's voice, using the beginning of each day to set priorities for that day, partnering with a colleague to help during really busy or stressful times.

8. Ask participants to discuss what gets in the way of their doing the above (#7) and what can be done to change that situation. (Note: Make sure participants take ownership of the changes and do not let this become a complaint session.)

Be sure to end on a positive note!

Examples of Reliability

Businesses that deliver consistently reliable service	
Why you do business with them	
Businesses whose service quality is erratic or unreliable	
Why you do or do not do business with them	

ACTIVITY **8**

Reliability: Promises, Promises

Reliability is doing what is promised dependably and accurately. A promise represents a sacred trust. Failing to live up to the promises we make to customers, even seemingly small commitments, can irreparably harm customer loyalty. Trust is the platinum standard of customer service, the precious metal that keeps customers coming back again and again. Where are the promises given by your organization?

PURPOSE:

 To recognize the different types of promises made by the organization

 To uncover the expectations that customers have of the organization and its employees

TIME: Two 20-minute meetings, one week of customer discovery

DIRECTIONS

1. Explain to participants that there are three types of promises: organizational, personal, and customer driven. Use Part A of Activity 8 to develop your discussion.

2. After explaining the three types of promises, ask participants what other examples of each type they can think of that relate to your organization.

3. Let participants know that someone can break a promise to a customer without even knowing it—for example, by being out of stock on an advertised item, not following up on a call to a customer, or assuming

a customer knows there are shipping charges even though it's not stated in an obvious way. It is important to uncover what each customer's expectations are.

4. Ask participants if they can think of a time when a customer expressed disappointment or when they were surprised by a customer's reaction to something they said.

5. State that the goal of the next several days is to uncover and gather customer expectations. When you come back together as a group you will compile what you have learned.

6. Ask participants how they might determine customer expectations. Look for answers like, "We can do a survey," "We can ask the customer in face-to-face encounters," "We can call customers for feedback."

7. Using Part B of Activity 8, develop some questions associates can use to solicit information from customers as to their expectations. Some examples include:

- When you call our department, what kind of service do you expect to get from us?

- Based on your history of business with our company, what service expectations do you have?

- Describe the level of service you expect to receive from us compared to our competitors.

- What dimension of our service quality is most important to you— for example, knowledgeable associates, timely support, keeping promises, effective problem solving?

- What are some of your assumptions about our products and how they will perform?

8. Ask the participants to commit to three to five customer contacts in the next five days. Remind them to keep notes on these contacts and be prepared to discuss what happened in a week's time. (Note: If there is a chance of overlap, ask participants to identify the customer contacts in advance so as to avoid duplication.) Distribute copies of Part C of Activity 8 so participants can keep notes.

9. At the follow-up meeting, ask participants to provide one example of what they learned. Good debriefing questions include:

- What did customers say that reinforced what you already knew?

- What new information did customers provide that is different from what you thought?

- What opinions did the customers give that might help the department do a better job in meeting their expectations?

- Did you find this experience to be positive or negative? What made it so?

- What was the reaction of your customers when you asked for their input?

- How does the customer input differ from what you thought the customer might expect?

10. At the end of the discussion, ask participants to summarize what the group has learned about customer expectations and how that knowledge differs from their previous assumptions.

11. With the information you have, ask participants what they might do to change, add, or eliminate behaviors to better meet the expectations of customers and deliver on the promises that have been made.

PART A

Use the following as resource material for developing the group discussion of kinds of promises.

- *Organizational* promises are stated obligations that appear in many forms: advertising and marketing materials, warranties or guarantees, Web sites, contracts.

- *Personal* promises are commitments made to or for customers, and these are the most common types of promises: "I'll call you back tomorrow," "I'll check on that," "I can have that done by next week," "I can help you with that."

- *Customer-driven* promises are implications that customer expectations will be met. These understandings impact how customers approach doing business with you, and can be based on their business history with your organization or on standard practice in the industry, or on general beliefs and assumptions. Examples include, "If I give you information related to my business, it is to be kept confidential," "If I bring my car in for service, you will do only what we agreed upon," "If I have gotten free delivery on appliances from a competitor, your company should have free delivery, too."

PART B

Questions to ask my customers:

1. _____
   _____
   _____

2. _____
   _____
   _____

3. _____
   _____
   _____

PART C

	Contact Log			
	Whom Did I Contact?	What Did I Learn?	What Surprised Me?	What Will I Do Differently?
Contact 1				
Contact 2				
Contact 3				
Contact 4				
Contact 5				

ACTIVITY 9

Reliability: Secret Shopper

Reliability is doing what is promised, dependably and accurately. Reliability occurs when both internal and external customers can count on the service they receive to be consistently stellar. Here, your participants become "secret shoppers" to observe the level of Reliability in other businesses.

PURPOSE:

✓ To observe what other businesses do to be Reliable

✓ To relate the performance of other businesses to your own business

✓ To heighten awareness of the importance of Reliability

TIME: 1 week, variable times

DIRECTIONS:

1. Identify businesses that associates have experienced as Reliable. (See Activity 7 or create a new list.)

2. Ask participants to identify two companies: one whose services they frequent regularly and one that is unfamiliar to them. Assign them to shop at various times during their business day. (Note: You may want to assign the same business to more than one person, so as to compare the shopping experiences. And you might want to use your competition as one of the businesses to shop.) Distribute two copies of Activity 9 to each participant so they can log their comments.

3. Determine what associates will look for when "secret shopping." List the attributes that customers experience as Reliable. Look for behaviors such as getting the same response from each person to the same question, having a person get back to the "shopper" after promising to check on something, observing if goods are consistently in stock, the location is clean, advertised merchandise is on hand.

4. Set a date for when the "secret shopping" will be completed.

5. At the appointed time, discuss what associates have experienced. Ask questions like:

- At each visit, what were your experiences regarding Reliability?
- How does the experience of one associate compare to that of another who visited the same business?
- What observations did you make that reinforced the factor of Reliability in delivering *Knock Your Socks Off Service?*
- What problems or breakdowns in Reliability did you experience?

6. After this discussion, ask participants how what they learned can be applied to your company and the product or service you provide. Make a plan to implement those suggestions.

Note: When scheduling visits to businesses outside your organization, allow associates to take some time away from work. This may mean their leaving early one day to get to the targeted business on the way home or arriving a bit later so associates may visit the business on the way to work. Remember, the goal is to "secret shop" the selected businesses at a variety of times.

Reliability is doing what is promised, dependably and accurately. Delivering on promises builds trust, the glue that holds business relationships together.

1. How did the company you shopped demonstrate Reliability?

_____

_____

_____

_____

2. If the company you shopped wasn't reliable in some way, how did it let you down and why?

_____

_____

_____

_____

3. How could Reliability have been improved at the location?

_____

_____

_____

_____

4. What did you learn about Reliability that can be applied at your organization?

_____

_____

_____

_____

Assurance: The Language of Competence

Assurance is the knowledge and courtesy you show to customers, and your ability to convey trust, confidence, and competence. When you are communicating with customers, your words can make a big difference in how you are perceived. Make yourself stand out with both a great attitude and skillful use of words and phrases that suggest a can-do, proactive service approach.

PURPOSE:

✓ To build a vocabulary of words and phrases that demonstrate competence and confidence

✓ To practice using these words in interactions with customers

TIME: 30 minutes

DIRECTIONS:

1. Copy and cut out the word cards for Part A of Activity 10 and give each group of participants a set. Ask them to put the cards in two stacks: one stack of words that send a message of confidence and the other with words that do not. Allow 3 to 4 minutes for this activity.

2. Ask each group to present its two stacks. (Note: You may want to use a wall or large white board, and have participants post their words for the group to see.)

3. Once all groups have presented their sortings, review the discrepancies and discuss the words to reach a consensus on meanings. There should be lively discussion about these words.

4. Ask participants to practice using the words in a couple of quick role-play situations; see Part B. For each situation there should be a customer, a service provider, and an observer—if you have enough people. Have the group rotate through each role, using the scenarios given. The observer should provide feedback to the service provider on the application of the words. The customer may also give feedback. Allow 10 to 12 minutes for all three role-plays.

5. Ask the participants the following questions:
   - How did this role-playing situation work for you?
   - What was the difference in the interactions with the customers?
   - For the customers, what was your comfort level with the service providers?
   - What did others do well?
   - What was difficult about this activity?
   - How do you feel about incorporating the "confidence words" on a regular basis into your interactions with customers?

6. Encourage participants to try using the words that convey confidence during the next week and be prepared to report back at the next meeting.

PART A

Photocopy the pages with the words and phrases to make as many sets as you need. Cut the "cards" apart so participants can sort them during the activity.

I hope. . .	I am confident. . .
I might. . .	I can. . .
In my experience. . .	I'm not sure. . .
I know. . .	Gee, let me see. . .

✂ -

I am going to need to check on that. . .	I think I need to transfer you. . .
I need to ask my supervisor. . .	I'd like to suggest. . .
Let me make sure I understand. . .	I can't do that.

This activity is available at: www.amacombooks.org/go/101ActDKYSOS
© 2009 AMACOM, a division of American Management Association.

Flash Card Categories (for Facilitators Only)

Demonstrates Confidence or Competence	Does Not Demonstrate Confidence or Competence
I am confident that…	I hope…
I can…	I might…
In my experience…	I'm not sure…
I know…	Gee, let me see…
I'd like to suggest…	I think I need to transfer you…
Let me make sure I understand…	I need to ask my supervisor…
I'm going to need to check on that…	I can't do that…

PART B

The following scenarios are suggested for role-play situations, or you may develop your own. These situations should challenge participants to use the words the group agrees best demonstrate competence and confidence.

* **Scenario 1.** A customer calls about an old item/part/piece and is very confused. She wants to replace/repair it, but doesn't think it's still available or can be repaired.

* **Scenario 2.** A customer is insistent that s/he has spoken to you in the past about a recurring problem regarding billing. But your department doesn't handle billing at all.

* **Scenario 3.** A customer is asking for a favor in getting a shipment out immediately. There are many other orders ahead of this customer's and the quantity is currently limited.

ACTIVITY **11**

Assurance: The Knowledge Game

Assurance is the knowledge and courtesy you show to customers, and your ability to convey trust, confidence, and competence. Assurance is best given to the customer through a demonstration of product knowledge, company knowledge, good listening skills, and problem-solving acumen. When your associates are well trained and confident in these areas, their confidence comes through loud and clear to customers as they experience the formidable combination of service style and substance.

PURPOSE:

✓ To learn and reinforce a knowledge of your company's products/services and its operations

✓ To have some fun and team-build while learning new skills

✓ To relate how product and service knowledge benefits the customer

TIME: 45 minutes

DIRECTIONS:

1. Since you will be setting up a game similar to the television show *Jeopardy*, some preparation will be necessary prior to the meeting. You'll need to use index cards to make up the "answers" that will serve as the questions in the game. On the cards, list specific product/service features, benefits to your customer of the features of your product/service, company departments or functional areas, skills of listening, and problem-solving skills. Try to create two levels of questions—easy and harder—with a total of 12 to 15 cards per round. More is better. Refer to the suggestions that follow.

2. Form two or more teams of participants. Mix the teams by experience level. Each team is asked a question by the moderator or meeting facilitator and has 10 seconds to answer it. If a team cannot answer the question correctly, the other team(s) has an opportunity to answer the same question.

3. Hold two rounds of questions and then ask a final, bonus question. Round 1 is for one point each. Round 2 is for two points each; the bonus question is worth five points. Each team has an opportunity to get points in the bonus round. The winning team–with the most points at the end of the session—is the winner.

4. As in the television game, the "answer" is posed and the team response is given in the form of a question. For example, suppose the "answer" is, "Who? What? When? Where? How?" The team response should be, "What are open-ended questions?" As another example, suppose the "answer" is, "Clarification on an invoice question." The team response might be, "Who is the Billing Department?" For yet another example, suppose the "answer" is, "Time and money savings." The team response might be, "What is a customer benefit for the XYZ product?"

5. Plan a reward for the group, to be shared at the end of the meeting. A fun award for the winning team also is a good idea. For example, purchase medals or make them with ribbons. Even a candy bar or 15-minute lunch extension would be great prizes. See if the winning team is challenged to a rematch!

Suggested "Answers" for Question Cards

1. *Listening skills.* Use phrases such as "asking open-ended questions," "closed-ended questions," "summarizing," "making eye contact," "note taking," "paraphrasing," "follow-up questions," "probing questions," "clarifying questions."

2. *Problem-solving skills.* Use phrases such as "suspending judgment until the customer is finished speaking," "listening completely to the customer," "involving the customer in solutions," "asking the customer how s/he would like a situation resolved," "offering options to the customer," "making suggestions to the customer."

3. *Product/service features*. These cards should have the specifics of your product or service—model numbers, delivery constraints or options, colors, sizes, features, pricing, guarantees or warranty information, and so on. The items need to be specific to your organization or work group and should reflect both minimum knowledge and mastery of product or service information.

4. *Benefits to your customer*. Based on the product features, list ways these benefit your customer—for example, why one model number over another? Why one shipping option vs. another? Why buy the more expensive item? Why should the customer have the extended warranty? Why upgrade? These phrases should always be stated in brief terms and reflect the best interests of the customers.

5. *Company knowledge*. On individual cards, list all the departments in your organization and their specific functions. List names of specific experts within those groups. Also on separate cards, list specific areas of expertise for the company—for example, how long have you been in business? Who is the president of the company? Where are all your offices located? Who is your biggest competition? What do you call your industry or category of business?

Alternative Versions of the Game

If you're feeling really creative, you can use this idea to make a game board, with flaps that open to reveal the answers behind them. Create as many categories as you want. Or, you can bypass the team structure and just read the answers and have the individuals respond. The point is to have some fun with this and make it a learning experience at the same time.

ACTIVITY **12**

Assurance: Secret Shopper

Assurance is the knowledge and courtesy you show to customers, and your ability to convey trust, confidence, and competence. What is inspirational is not what you do, but what you learn from others. How does your competition demonstrate Assurance? What are other organizations that are recognized for their competence and trust-building skills doing that you may not be doing? We can learn much from those who have mastered the art of Assurance.

PURPOSE:

✓ To observe the skills of other organizations in demonstrating Assurance

✓ To involve associates in observing the trust-building skills of other service providers in the organization

✓ To apply these observations to skills development in your organization

TIME: Two meetings—one 10 minutes, another 20 minutes; observation, variable time

DIRECTIONS:

1. Spend a few minutes discussing the businesses that participants believe have mastered the art of demonstrating Assurance. Some examples might include Lands' End, L.L. Bean, Amazon.com, Starbucks, the Container Store, Wegmans market. Ask about outstanding companies in your industry as well.

2. Explain to the participants that one great way to learn what others are doing well in the area of Assurance is to take on the role of "secret shopper." Explain that this is your goal for the next several days— to challenge and observe how other service providers assure their customers.

3. Ask participants how they think a secret shopper should think and act. Listen for answers like "Ask more challenging questions," "Ask for more detail than one would normally seek," "Make notes about what other service providers say or do well to make the customer trust them or see how they demonstrate their knowledge," "Put a service provider in a challenging situation to see how he uses problem-solving skills."

4. From your list of outstanding business examples, ask participants to pick two organizations they will contact in the next week, either by phone or in person. Using Activity 12, ask them to keep detailed notes of what the service providers say and do. Remind them of the need to focus on the skills that demonstrate Assurance.

5. At the follow-up meeting, have the participants share their observations, both positive and negative. Keep a list of both on separate charts.

6. Review the list of negative points and remind everyone that these behaviors are what they should avoid!

7. Review the list of positive points and ask the group how these skills or attributes can be incorporated into the work they do. Ask each person to commit to making one change in behavior and adding one skill to their knowledge base.

Assurance is the knowledge and courtesy you show to customers, and your ability to convey trust, confidence, and competence.

1. What did the service professional do that impressed you?

_____

_____

_____

_____

2.   What did the service professional do that disappointed you?

   _____

   _____

   _____

   _____

3.   How did the service professional gain your trust and, ultimately, lead you to trust the product or service?

   _____

   _____

   _____

   _____

4.   What did you learn from your interaction with the service professional?

   _____

   _____

   _____

   _____

My Personal Commitment

I, _____, personally commit to changing the following behavior _____,
and to make _____ a regular part of my working with customers on a daily basis.

Signed_____   Date_____

Tangibles: Take a Field Trip

Tangibles are the physical facilities, equipment, and appearance of service personnel, that can help make the intangible elements of service memorable and satisfying to customers. If you have ever put your hands down on a sticky counter at a fast-food restaurant or dealt with a service worker who smells like cigarette smoke, you know just how important such elements of service can be. If you can hear it, see it, smell it, taste it, or touch it, it's a Tangible. We call this the Tangible factor, the third of the RATER factors.

PURPOSE:

✔ To heighten awareness of the Tangibles in your workplace

✔ To shift perspective to the customer's point of view on Tangibles

TIME: 30 minutes

DIRECTIONS:

1. When the group is gathered, remind them of what Tangibles are all about.

2. Describe what is going to happen on your field trip. As you navigate your work space, area, or building, ask participants to consider what they see, hear, touch, smell, and possibly taste that the customers (both external and internal) will also experience. You want participants to experience these Tangibles through the customers' eyes. Encourage the participants to take notes as they walk around and observe. Distribute copies of Activity 13.

3. Lead the group outside your building, then move back inside and make your way back to your work space. Ask the following questions along the way to get participants thinking about what they observe on the field trip.

- What do you see? How does the exterior present itself?

- What reactions or feelings might that exterior elicit from customers? What does the exterior of the building say about our organization?

- How are people greeted as they enter the building? What do they hear, see, smell?

- What signage is there to direct people to where they want to go? If you didn't know anything about the company, could you find the department or people you wanted to talk with?

- If you take an elevator, what guides are posted to help you find the department or person you are looking for?

- How tidy or clean are the work spaces?

- What is the background noise you hear?

- How inviting is the work area for a visit from an internal or external customer?

- What signs or directories are in place to guide you to the work area or to a specific person?

4. Once back from your field trip, debrief the participants. Start with the big picture and work toward a detailed view. Some of the following questions may help:

- What is the overall perception an external customer may develop about our organization as a result of the exterior presentation?

- What do people hear as they come into the building?

- How clear and appropriate is the signage in the building?

- For our internal customers, what do they experience upon first entering our department or area?

5. Ask participants how these obvious Tangibles might be changed to bring about the perception you want customers to have about the company or department.

Field Trip Log

	Positive Impressions?	Negative Impressions?	What Do Customers See?	What Do You Want Them to See?
Parking lot				
Exterior of building				
Elevator				
Reception				
Work space				
Signage				

Tangibles: Sensory Perception

Tangibles are the physical facilities, equipment, and appearance of service personnel. Tangibles come into play before, during, and after service interactions and have a big influence on customers' perceptions of your organization. Some of these factors you can control, some you can't. The idea is to focus on the Tangibles you can control or improve.

PURPOSE:

✓ To identify all of the Tangibles that are part of the work you do

✓ To consider each Tangible and how it impacts customers' perceptions

✓ To modify where necessary any Tangible that may lead to a negative perception

TIME: 30 minutes

DIRECTIONS:

1. Remind participants what makes up a Tangible.

2. Divide the participants into groups of three or four each. Distribute copies of Activity 14 to facilitate a brainstorming session.

3. Ask participants to list all the Tangibles that are part of their work, placing them into the five "sense" categories. Allow 5 to 7 minutes.

4. While participants are working, post five chart pads for recording purposes. Mark each with a heading for one of the five senses (parallel to the columns on their paper).

5. Working with one category at a time, ask participants to identify and categorize all the Tangibles.

6. Lead a discussion with the participants, using the following questions:
   - Which of these Tangibles are completely within your control?
   - How likely is it that this Tangible impacts the customer (remember both internal and external customers) and to what degree?
   - What perception might the customer develop as a result of this Tangible?
   - What might we/you do to change or improve that Tangible?

7. Ask participants to determine which Tangibles need to be improved first, given their impact on customer satisfaction.

8. Build a plan to prioritize those improvements and make them. Set a time frame for completion or the expectation of changed behavior.

9. Check on participants' progress in making these goals.

Examples of Workplace Tangibles				
Hear	See	Smell	Taste	Touch

ACTIVITY 15

Tangibles: Customer Feedback

Tangibles are the physical facilities, equipment, and appearance of service personnel. Customers have a lot to say about the Tangibles they experience. Tangibles are just that—easy to see and easy to criticize. To ensure that your company's Tangibles meet or exceed your customers' expectations, ask for their input.

PURPOSE:

✓ To learn more about customers' perceptions of the Tangibles they experience

✓ To identify ways to improve these Tangibles based on customer input

✓ To build better relationships with your customers

TIME: Two meetings—one 10-minutes, one 30-minutes; contact time during work days for one week

DIRECTIONS:

1. When the group is assembled, remind them of what Tangibles are. (If you have conducted Activity 14, consider using the charts you created as a starting point here.)

2. Identify one or two key Tangibles that all customers experience. If you deal regularly with both external and internal customers, you may want to select one for each type.

3. Explain to participants that the goal for the next several days is to gather specific feedback from your customers on this particular

Tangible. You may decide to create a short "script" for people to use in explaining the feedback process to customers and to tell them how important their feedback is to the company. Be sure to include an enthusiastic thank-you at the end of the discussion with each customer. Write the script as provided in Part A of the activity.

4. Distribute copies of Part B of Activity 15. Ask participants to speak with a minimum of two customers to solicit feedback on the specific Tangible identified above. If there is likelihood that several participants will contact the same business or individuals, ask them to decide which customers each will solicit so there is no duplication.

5. At the follow-up meeting, ask participants to summarize the feedback they received from the customers. Keep track of both positive and negative feedback.

6. Summarize what the participants have said. As a group, decide what change you will make about the Tangible surveyed. Ask if a particular participant wishes to make this change and offer it for group review.

Note: There are a variety of ways to conduct this exercise. When soliciting client feedback, you can also start by asking customers what they consider the most important Tangibles. This allows you to focus on those Tangibles that have the greatest impact on customer loyalty. Making improvements in your service based on feedback builds significant goodwill with customers, as they can see their input put into practice.

PART A

Create a script to use when contacting customers.

_____

_____

_____

_____

_____

_____

PART B

Tangible 1: _____

Contact Log

	Whom Did I Contact?	What Did I Learn?	What Surprised Me?	What Will I Do Differently?
Contact 1				
Contact 2				
Contact 3				
Contact 4				
Contact 5				

Tangible 2: _____

Contact Log

	Whom Did I Contact?	What Did I Learn?	What Surprised Me?	What Will I Do Differently?
Contact 1				
Contact 2				
Contact 3				
Contact 4				
Contact 5				

Tangibles: Secret Shopper

Tangibles are the physical facilities, equipment, and appearance of service personnel. Pay attention to the details, and your organization can leave your customers Wowed! You can learn much from others on ways to improve and leave your positive, lasting impression.

PURPOSE:

✓ To observe how much other organizations pay attention to the Tangibles

✓ To apply these observations to Tangibles in your organization

TIME: Two meetings—one 10 minutes, one 20 minutes; observation time varies

DIRECTIONS:

1. Spend a few minutes discussing those businesses that your associates believe focus on the details of the Tangibles. Some examples of businesses that pay attention to details are Disney theme parks, Wegmans market, and Ritz-Carlton hotels. Ask participants for examples in your industry as well.

2. Explain to the participants that one great way to learn what others do well is to become a "secret shopper." As was done for the two earlier RATER factors, secret shopping is the goal of the next several days: challenging other service providers to pay attention to the details and observing the results.

3. Ask participants how they will become secret shoppers—what might they do or ask to find out how well other companies pay attention to details? Listen for responses like, "Ask more challenging questions," "Ask for more detail than one would normally seek," "Make notes about what other organizations do to focus on details," "Review signage, printed materials, and work areas that demonstrate commitment to detail."

4. From your list of businesses, ask the participants to each pick two organizations they will contact in the next week, either by phone or in person. Ask the participants to keep detailed notes of what Tangibles they observe. Remind them that their focus is on Tangibles and how these service providers demonstrate sensitivity to customers' experiences, especially with their senses—hearing, seeing, smelling, tasting, touching. Distribute two copies of Activity 16 to each participant.

5. At the follow-up meeting, ask participants to share their observations, both positive and negative. Keep a list of these observations on separate chart papers, one for positive and one for negative.

6. Review the list of negative points and remind everyone that these are factors you want to avoid!

7. Review the list of positive points and ask the group how this close attention to Tangibles might be incorporated into the work they do. Ask each person to commit to making one change in behavior and one addition to his or her skill set.

Tangibles—the physical facilities and equipment, and the appearance of personnel. If you can hear it, see it, smell it, taste it, or touch it, it's a Tangible.

1. What appealed to you about the exterior of the facility?

   _____

2. How did it affect your expectations of your visit?

   _____

3. What Tangibles could have been different (good or bad) to change your impression?

   _____

4. How did the service person deal with the Tangibles around him or her?

   _____

Empathy vs. Sympathy

Empathy is seeing things from the customer's perspective; acknowledging their feelings and situation. This ability is one of the most important skills to master in the realm of customer service. The degree to which you show your customers caring and individual attention can make a satisfied customer become a loyal customer. In this world of high-tech and automation, customers really crave high touch!

PURPOSE:

✓ To differentiate between Empathy and sympathy

✓ To see the value of Empathy in dealing with customers

TIME: 20 minutes; pair this activity with Activity 18 for additional practice.

DIRECTIONS:

1. Ask participants when they have experienced a service provider who took the time to understand their needs, wants, or expectations—who created a memorable experience.

2. Ask all participants to reflect on what made those experiences memorable. Listen for responses such as, "The service provider asked good questions," "The service provider took time with the customer," "The service provider demonstrated an understanding of the feelings of the customer."

3. Open up a discussion of the difference between Empathy and sympathy. You may want to start with this situation: A customer calls who is

clearly angry because she has been cut off once and transferred to at least one or more departments. Which response is likely to connect better with the customer?

- "I understand how you feel."
- "It's clear to me that you are frustrated with how your call has been handled."

Explain that one of these statements represents sympathy and the other represents Empathy. Present the group with a chart based on Activity 17. Distribute copies of the definitions based on Activity 17 and direct participants to discuss the difference between these two words. Emphasize that Empathy involves making a personal connection with the customer. It is not demeaning, belittling, or diminishing the customer in any way; rather, it is using words that identify the emotion and capture the basic message. It shows that you are focused on the customer and hear and appreciate what the individual is saying. Explain that when associates respond with sympathy, that response puts them emotionally where the customer is. It is, more often than not, unproductive. But when they respond with Empathy, they stay emotionally calm and in control while, at the same time, recognizing and validating the emotional state of the customer.

4. End the discussion with some of the following conclusions:

- Empathy does not mean saying "I'm sorry" or taking ownership.
- Empathy keeps the focus on the customer.
- Empathy helps the service provider stay calm and in control of the conversation.
- Empathy tells the customer that s/he is valued and attention is being paid to the problem.
- Empathy takes practice and showing Empathy is not always easy, especially when customers are angry.
- Empathy adds the human touch to service.
- Empathy is the memory-making experience in great service.

5. Encourage participants to see frustrated and angry customers as opportunities for showing how much you care. Get participants to understand how showing Empathy can change the outcome of the interaction.

Empathy vs. Sympathy Definitions

Sympathy

Identifying with and taking on the other person's emotion

Example:
"I'm really angry about the delay in confirmation, too."

Empathy

Acknowledging and affirming the other person's emotional state

Example:
"It's clear to me that you are angry about the delay in the confirmation. That is aggravating."

"*The more high tech the world becomes,
the more people crave high-touch service.*"
—JOHN NAISBITT
Megatrends: 10 New Directions for Transforming Our Lives

Empathy: Building a Statement

Empathy is seeing things from the customer's perspective; acknowledging their feelings and situation. The degree to which you show your customers caring and individual attention can make a satisfied customer become a loyal customer. Empathy takes some practice; your comments need to be genuine and sincere. Practice makes proficient.

PURPOSE:

✔ To reinforce the value of a well-placed Empathy statement

✔ To build an Empathy statement

✔ To hear what an Empathy statement sounds like and the feelings it provokes

TIME: 20 minutes

DIRECTIONS:

1. Remind participants what an Empathy statement is. Explain that the ability to show Empathy often does not come easily to people. Also point out that when a service provider shows Empathy, the customer may not be aware of this as a service provider's special skill.

2. Distribute copies of Activity 18 and review the steps involved in building an Empathy statement. Offer some examples of statements that apply in the work environment, including, "I can hear how frustrated you are over this confusion," "It is clear that you are disappointed with the replacement item," "I can see that you are confused by the different options I have suggested."

3. Ask for a volunteer. Based on the volunteer's job, offer a complaint or concern that a customer might make, and have the volunteer reply with an Empathy statement as part of the response. As guidance, post the "Build a Statement of Empathy" steps (Part A, Activity 18) for the group to refer to during the practice. For example, say to the volunteer, "I really don't like this new process for ordering." The volunteer's response might be, "It seems to me that you are frustrated by the change in process." Remember that it is unlikely the volunteer will give a good Empathy response the first time. This is a great opportunity to thank the volunteer and use the group to work on structuring the Empathy statement so that it will work.

4. Continue this process until everyone in the group has had an opportunity to practice an Empathy statement.

5. OPTIONAL: Should you find that participants are having a hard time identifying and acknowledging a customer's emotion, try listing words often used to describe emotions. Point out that we have five basic emotions—mad, sad, glad, afraid, and guilty. Start with mad, and ask, "How many different words or phrases do we use to say 'mad?'" Providing the vocabulary can help participants better label the emotions.

6. OPTIONAL: If time allows, ask participants to pair up to jointly write an Empathy statement that can be used in a typical situation they face on the job. Have the partners read them aloud to the group for all to benefit. Use Part B of Activity 18 to complete this option.

PART **A**

Build a Statement of Empathy

Lead-in

- I hear that…
- I see that…
- It's clear to me that…

Acknowledgment of the other person

- You…
- I hear that you…

Description of the feelings

- Angry, frustrated, anxious, disappointed, nervous, confused, surprised, thrilled
- I hear that you are angry…

Description of the situation

- Because… [content of the message]
- I hear that you are angry because the shipment will be late.

PART **B**

Your Model Statement. Create your Empathy statement:

_____

_____

_____

_____

_____

Empathy:
Scripting Tough Situations

Empathy is seeing things from the customer's perspective; acknowledging their feelings and situation. Showing Empathy is one of the most important skills to master in the realm of customer service. Customers come in a wide variety of shapes and sizes, and they bring an equally wide variety of wants, needs, expectations, attitudes, and emotions to the service transaction. Most important, customers want to be treated as individuals. Even so, there are customer situations that come up repeatedly. It's great to have some ready expressions for dealing with these regular occurrences.

PURPOSE:

✓ To identify recurring tough situations

✓ To plan how to handle them

✓ To script responses that build confidence and knowledge

TIME: 20 minutes

DIRECTIONS:

1. Ask participants, in small groups, to list tough situations that come up repeatedly. Allow 3 to 4 minutes.

2. Have each group report on its list. As you hear the descriptions, list them for everyone to see. If a situation is cited by more than one group, put check marks (✓) in front of it to show its repetition.

3. Ask participants what their comfort level is when handling these situations.

4. Explain that there may be several ways to handle these situations, and that this is the focus of the meeting. Explain that they will be scripting responses to these situations. The scripts will begin with the Empathy statement because it dictates how the interaction proceeds. Remind participants that the scripting isn't to come up with statements that can be read to customers; rather, it will provide more ways of expressing Empathy with customers.

5. Hand out copies of Activity 19 and ask that each group pick one situation to work on. Make sure each group is working on a different situation. Allow 4 to 5 minutes.

6. Ask each group to present its script.

7. After the presentations are completed, ask if one person would be willing to collect the forms and compile a set for everyone to have. (Note: Keep your list of tough situations as you may want to work on others in the future.)

This example will show how the script is to be prepared.

Example

Situation: Partial shipment on an order. Customer calls in angry, wanting to know when the rest of the order will be sent.

Empathy Statements	Options for Resolution	Thank the Customer
"It is really frustrating when orders don't arrive as expected."	• Ship immediately at your cost • Substitute an available item • Ask customer if a partial shipment of the item would be okay now with the balance to be sent in xxx days.	"I am really glad you called to let me know this happened."

Script Your Own

Your Situation: _____

_____

Empathy Statements	Options for Resolution	Thank the Customer

This activity is available at: www.amacombooks.org.go:101ActDKYSOS
© 2009 AMACOM. a division of American Management Association.

ACTIVITY **20**

Empathy: Partnering for Practice

Empathy is seeing things from the customer's perspective; acknowledging their feelings and situation. Empathy is a critical skill to master for *Knock Your Socks Off Service*. Practice makes us proficient and confident. Customers appreciate personal attention demonstrated by caring, knowledgeable professionals. Connecting on an emotional level provides the kind of service that customers are likely to long remember and cherish.

PURPOSE:

✓ To increase skill and comfort level when making Empathy statements

✓ To give and accept feedback [from an associate]

TIME: 15 minutes

DIRECTIONS:

1. Remind participants of any prior discussion you have had about Empathy—its power and value.

2. Quickly review the steps to "Building a Statement of Empathy" (see Part A, Activity 18).

3. Explain to participants that proficiency in this exercise will improve their comfort level when showing Empathy. Ask participants to identify an associate with whom they are willing to practice and give and get feedback.

4. Prepare the flash cards in Activity 20 and use the "quick draw" situations to have participants respond with an Empathy statement. Give each pair a set of cards to draw from the deck for practice. Allow 6 to 7 minutes. If they finish, have them mix the cards and start again. Remind participants that after each round they should give each other some quick feedback:

- How did the Empathy statement make you feel as the customer?
- Did giving the Empathy statement come easily?
- What was difficult about saying that?
- How did being empathetic change your comfort level?

5. Reassemble the group for a discussion of feedback. You are likely to hear that being empathetic was hard and seemed artificial. Ask participants the following questions to stress the value of this skill:

- How can this skill be put into practice on the job?
- How will you be able to further practice this skill prior to using it with customers?
- When you were the "customer," how did receiving an Empathy response make them feel?

6. Ask the pairs if they will continue to work with each other on the job. The goal here is for the partners to listen to each other a couple of times a week and continue to provide feedback on their Empathy skills.

Copy the following pages and cut them apart following the lines so you have "quick draw" flash-card situations for the practice.

I don't like those shipping options.

I have been waiting for someone to get back to me.

Does anyone in your organization know what is going on?

I just want my report on time!

How many people do I need to talk to before I get an answer?

Look, I just need my product sent.

You mean you can really help me?

I love doing business with your company.

The sign says service department! If you can't help me, who can?

That's just not acceptable!

Look, I'm not sure if I have the right department or not.

I really need this back immediately. Tomorrow isn't good enough.

My system is down yet again!

I always get the best people when I call your company.

ACTIVITY **21**

Responsiveness: Identifying the Barriers

Responsiveness is the willingness to help and provide prompt service. It's about follow-up and follow-through, finding the answer rather than transferring your customer to someone else. It's keeping the customer informed of your progress, about establishing priorities and deadlines. It's about delivering bad news before the customer has to ask.

PURPOSE:

✓   To uncover the real and imagined barriers to Responsiveness

✓   To problem-solve to remove or reduce barriers to Responsiveness

✓   To identify how customers appreciate Responsiveness

TIME: 30 minutes

DIRECTIONS:

1. Prior to the meeting, copy and cut out the "barriers" flash cards in Part A of Activity 21. You will want one set for each small group.

2. Explain to participants what Responsiveness is in the RATER factors.

3. Ask participants to think about and describe a time when they waited for a response from someone—an internal customer, a doctor, an airline, another service provider. Select two or three examples, and use the following questions to draw out key points:

    •   What happened to your emotions as you waited for a response?

- What was your sense of control in the situation?
- Who had to initiate the follow-up?
- What similarities did you hear in these examples?

4. Explain that often there are real or imagined barriers to providing good service to your customers. In small groups, ask participants to rank the barriers they believe are problems for them. Tell them they will be given a group of index cards with some barriers written on them and a couple of blank cards to list some additional barriers. Allow 4 to 5 minutes.

5. Call time and tell the groups they have one minute to pick their top two barriers in their stack of cards. It's okay if the groups select the same barriers, as their solutions are likely to be different.

6. Now, it is time to do some problem solving. Distribute copies of Part B of Activity 21 and ask the groups to come up with suggestions for eliminating or reducing the barriers. You may need or want to set parameters to exclude some solutions, such as, "There is no additional money for new hires." Allow 8 to 10 minutes. Have the groups record their suggestions for collection at the end of the session.

7. Call time and ask the groups to briefly present their solutions. Collect the papers for review and implementation wherever possible.

PART A

Not Enough Time	Not Enough People
Not Enough Information	Unrealistic Deadlines
No Respect from Other Departments	Poor Communication Between Departments

PART B

1. Identify your top two barriers:

   _____

   _____

   _____

2. How can we eliminate or reduce these barriers?

   _____

   _____

   _____

ACTIVITY **22**

Responsiveness: Proactive vs. Reactive

Responsiveness is the willingness to help and provide prompt service. It requires being proactive with customers rather than reactive. When we reduce the number of surprises the customer experiences, we are more in control of the conversation. You're even likely to get a "thank you" for the information.

PURPOSE:

✓ To be clear about the difference between being proactive and reactive

✓ To learn and understand why being proactive is important

✓ To identify ways to improve Responsiveness in the department

TIME: 20 minutes

DIRECTIONS:

1. Remind participants what the Responsiveness factor is about.

2. Distribute all four scenarios of Activity 22. In small groups, have them read the scenarios and answer the questions for each one. Allow 8 to 10 minutes.

3. Reassemble the group and work through each of the scenarios, discussing each one.

4. Ask participants how they might incorporate the discussion topics from this activity into their daily routines with customers.

SITUATION 1

One of your good, and regular, customers has placed an order for a number of items to replenish his stock. During that call, he indicated that there was no immediate rush, so standard shipping was selected. The order is due to ship in a couple of days. Today, the warehouse manager sent an e-mail alert that one of your top-selling items is on back order. (There was some mix-up from your supplier.) You know this item is on your customer's order. Knowing the order is not critical, you decide not to contact your customer. A few days later, he is on the phone asking where his product is.

1. Is this response by the service provider proactive or reactive?

   _____

   _____

2. How might you change this situation?

   _____

   _____

3. What might the customer be thinking about your organization?

   _____

   _____

SITUATION 2

The phone lines have just opened for the day. You answer a call from a screaming customer who demands to know where her order is. "It was due in yesterday," she says. "I demand a credit for this order and want my next order shipped express for the cost of standard shipment." Every time you ask her for information that will help you research this situation, she cuts you off and starts yelling again. After a couple of great Empathy statements, you get the customer to agree to give you the important information. As you research this shipment, you tell her that the truck should be pulling up to her loading dock as you speak. You ask if she is willing to check this out. She agrees. You tell her you will call her back to check in. Fifteen minutes later, you call the customer back to confirm that the shipment has arrived. At that time, because of the delay in arrival, you offer the customer a 10 percent discount on her next order. Not only is she thrilled with the discount, but says she is shocked that you followed up as promised.

1. Is this response by the service provider proactive or reactive?

    _____

    _____

2. How might you change this situation?

    _____

    _____

3. What might the customer be thinking about your organization?

    _____

    _____

SITUATION 3

One of your internal customers has asked you to pull together some numbers for a meeting he will be attending. It will be easy for you to do that, so of course you say yes. The meeting is this Friday. The customer has asked to have the information by noon on Wednesday so he can review it and use it for some other reports. As you start to clean up your desk on Wednesday to go home, you realize you didn't get the work done for this customer. "Oh, well," you think, "I'll call him first thing tomorrow morning. It'll only take me about thirty minutes to get it done for him. I'm sure this will be sufficient." When you arrive the next morning, there is a terse e-mail waiting for you from the customer.

1. Is this response by the service provider proactive or reactive?

    _____

    _____

This activity is available at: www.amacombooks.org/go/101ActDKYSOS
© 2009 AMACOM, a division of American Management Association.

2. How might you change this situation?

_____

_____

3. What might the customer be thinking about your organization?

_____

_____

SITUATION 4

As a part of the daily routine, you are checking the order summary for orders received yesterday. You see something that looks unusual. One of your customers has an order placed for an odd quantity on one item. You ask the rep who took the order, and she confirms this is indeed what the customer ordered. Still perplexed, you decide to call the customer to confirm the quantity. When you talk to the customer, it is just as you suspected. The customer wants 240 pieces, not 240 dozen of this item. Laughing together about what a surprise that would have been upon delivery, you thank the customer for his time.

1. Is this response by the service provider proactive or reactive?

_____

_____

2. How might you change this situation?

_____

_____

3. What might the customer be thinking about your organization?

_____

_____

ACTIVITY **23**

Responsiveness: Role-Play

Responsiveness is the willingness to help and provide prompt service. Using the skills involved in Responsiveness will help us better serve customers. Practice makes us proficient. Here's some practice for providing information, delivering bad news, getting the answers to questions, and following up when you say you will.

PURPOSE:

✔ To practice determining customer expectations

✔ To experience how easy it is to negotiate with customers

✔ To learn how important Responsiveness is to customers

TIME: 30 minutes

DIRECTIONS:

1. Use the situations in Activity 23 or create your own. Make copies of the situations for the participants and divide them into two groups, for customers or service providers.

2. Review all the aspects of Responsiveness. Suggest that the best way for them to experience the value of Responsiveness is to deal with customers and see the results.

3. Divide the group into pairs. Explain that they will role-play as follows:

- Each pair will be given a situation. Person A will be the customer; Person B will be the service provider. The pairs switch roles for each role-play.

- They will have 3 to 4 minutes for the role-play, followed by 1 to 2 minutes for feedback.

- The goal of the role-play is to work out a mutually acceptable solution in a short amount of time. The primary focus here is on Responsiveness. Stress that participants use empathy, questioning, listening, problem solving, and negotiation to reach the resolution.

- After resolving the situation, the customer provides feedback to the service provider on how responsive the person was.

4. Distribute the first role-play and get them started. Watch the time and keep the group on track. Mingle and listen while making suggestions for improvement and ways to move the dialogue ahead. Call time and distribute the next role-play, this time reversing the roles.

5. Following the rounds of role-plays, ask the group the following questions:

- How did this exercise go?

- What did you learn?

- How did it feel to negotiate an outcome with your partner?

- What did people do well?

- How can this learning experience be incorporated into your regular work?

SITUATION 1

- **Customer.** You have just completed a phone call with one of your regular customers. There seems to be some confusion over a billing error. Your initial instinct was to transfer the call to the Billing Department. At that suggestion, the customer quickly states that she had been trying to work with Billing, but was getting nowhere. No one would call back. No one seemed to grasp the problem. So, she asked you to intervene. You agreed. You are off to talk to the Billing representative. You are now in the role of the customer! You would like an answer by the end of the day today, as this has been going on for a couple of weeks.

- **Service Provider.** Your colleague in the Service Department has just arrived to ask you about an external customer billing mix-up. As she explains the situation, you feel frustrated. The problem is not on your end, but on the external customer's side. You need additional information to resolve this problem and the customer hasn't provided that for you. Your colleague is convinced the problem is on our end and is demanding to have this cleared up by the end of the day. "After all," she says, "it's been going on for a couple of weeks now." You want to comply, but can't. You need more information from the customer, and once you have that, it will take a day to follow the process and figure out where the glitch is.

SITUATION 2

- **Customer.** As the shipping coordinator for your company, you are off to meet with a customer service rep about an order. It seems that the most recent order for a customer is just over the shipping weight limit for standard shipping. You would like the service rep to contact the customer to see how else to ship the order. There will be a cost increase for the customer, of course. And this is not the first time this has happened with this rep. You are pretty rigid about staying within guidelines for shipping to control your costs.

- **Service Provider.** The shipping coordinator has come to meet with you about a shipping concern. It seems that the most recent order you placed for one of your customers is just over the weight restrictions for standard shipping. The coordinator wants to have you call the customer and find out how else to ship the order. There seems to be a significant price increase the customer is going to incur with any change. This is one of your very regular and good customers. And, you have already accepted the order. You really don't want to call the customer now and change this. This shipping coordinator is a real "rule follower" and just doesn't make any exceptions.

SITUATION 3

- **Customer.** Frustrated by the phone queue at the company, you finally get a live human. Initially ecstatic, you realize that you need to talk to Stan, as you have had prior conversations with him. You ask to be transferred. The service rep you are talking to doesn't want to do that. You keep insisting. Ultimately, you just want to have your problem solved, which is to get a reference number for your bank. And, you need that now!

This activity is available at: www.amacombooks.org/go/101ActDKYSOS
© 2009 AMACOM, a division of American Management Association.

- **Service Provider.** A frustrated customer is on the phone demanding to talk to Stan. "I need to talk to Stan. He's the only one who can help me!" Stan is not available, so you want to help. The customer is not making this very easy for you.

SITUATION 4

- **Customer.** You are at the store, shopping for a GPS (Global Positioning System) for your car. You really don't know much about the assortment that is available, so you start asking questions of the floor salesperson. Quickly you assess that this young man has limited knowledge of the inventory. You are just about to walk away when another salesperson intervenes.

- **Service Provider.** You overhear one of your colleagues working with a customer who is shopping for a GPS for his vehicle. It's clear to you that your associate is not well versed on this product line. This puts you in a difficult situation, as you shouldn't "butt in," but you really don't want to lose the customer. And being sensitive to your associate, you don't want to make him look bad in front of the customer. You decide to approach the two of them.

> "*Customers perceive service in their own unique, idiosyncratic, emotional, irrational, end-of-the-day, and totally human terms. Perception is all there is!*"
> —Tom Peters

ACTIVITY 24

RATER Self-Assessment

It's helpful to have a framework that captures the multiple factors that determine the quality of a customer's service experience with your company. This is a self-assessment tool.

PURPOSE:

✓ To assess individual skill level in each of the RATER factors

✓ To build a plan to make changes and improvements in each RATER area

✓ To identify real-time behaviors that put meaning behind each RATER factor

TIME: 30–40 minutes

DIRECTIONS:

1. Copy and distribute one complete assessment form to each participant for Activity 24.

2. Instruct participants to follow the directions at the beginning of the assessment. Allow 25 to 30 minutes for completion.

3. When time is up, reassemble participants and use the following questions for debriefing:
   - What new awareness did you gain?
   - What is one example of an area needing improvement?
   - What surprised you?

RATER Self-Assessment

1. Part 1 of each section contains five statements that describe behaviors or actions associated with quality service for the factor being assessed. After reading each statement, circle the number that best describes how often you use the behavior described, using the following scale:

   Never = 0, Seldom = 1, Sometimes = 2, Usually = 3, and Always = 4.

2. If you feel your response would be different for internal vs. external customers, use two different-colored pens, one for internal customers and another for external customers. If a statement does not apply to your work situation, substitute an applicable behavior statement.

3. In Part 2, Action Plan, create a plan that will help you to deliver *Knock Your Socks Off Service*. Column A contains the same behavior descriptions used in Part 1. Start by setting a goal for behaviors you rated as 0, 1, or 2 and skip the behaviors you rated as 3 or 4.

4. In Column B, list the actions you will take to meet the service goals you set for yourself in Part 1.

5. In Column C, enter the target dates for completing your actions. Tip: Set realistic target dates—ones that are challenging but achievable.

6. In Column D, make notes about your progress. Review your action plans regularly—say, weekly or monthly—and note the status of each action and completion date. These reviews will remind you of the RATER factors and help you meet your goals for *Knock Your Socks Off Service*.

7. In six months to a year, retake the assessment and identify areas in which you've improved. Congratulate yourself and look for places where you can continue to improve.

Section I. Reliability

Part 1. Self-Assessment					
Reliability Behavior	Never	Seldom	Sometimes	Usually	Always
1. I keep promises I make to customers (e.g., return phone calls when promised, keep appointments).	0	1	2	3	4
2. My work is accurate.	0	1	2	3	4
3. I meet deadlines.	0	1	2	3	4
4. When I discover a service problem, I take the initiative to correct the situation.	0	1	2	3	4
5. The quality of my work meets or exceeds customers' expectations.	0	1	2	3	4

This activity is available at: www.amacombooks.org/go/101ActDKYSOS
© *2009 AMACOM, a division of American Management Association.*

Part 2. Action Plan

A. Reliability Behavior	B. Steps to Achieve My Goal	C. Target Date	D. Completion Date
1. I keep promises I make to customers (e.g., return phone calls when promised, keep appointments).			
2. My work is accurate.			
3. I meet deadlines.			
4. When I discover a service promise has been broken, I take the initiative to correct the situation.			
5. The quality of my work meets or exceeds customers' expectations.			

Section II. Assurance

Part 1. Self-Assessment					
Assurance Behavior	Never	Seldom	Sometimes	Usually	Always
1. I communicate a "can do" attitude to my customers by acting positive, confident, and helpful.	0	1	2	3	4
2. When a customer has a problem, I know how to fix things fast.	0	1	2	3	4
3. I can explain the features and benefits of our products and services to customers.	0	1	2	3	4
4. I can explain the organization's policies to customers.	0	1	2	3	4
5. If a customer's needs fall outside my area of responsibility, I guide the customer to someone who can help.	0	1	2	3	4

Part 2. Action Plan

A. Assurance Behavior	B. Steps to Achieve My Service Goal	C. Target Date	D. Completion Date
1. I communicate a "can do" attitude to my customers by acting positive, confident, and helpful.			
2. When a customer has a problem, I know how to fix things fast.			
3. I can explain the features and benefits of our products and services to customers.			
4. I can explain the organization's policies to customers.			
5. If a customer's needs fall outside my area of responsibility, I guide the customer to someone who can help.			

Section III. Tangibles

Part 1. Self-Assessment					
Tangibles Behavior	Never	Seldom	Sometimes	Usually	Always
1. When I can be seen by customers, I am dressed neatly and appropriately.	0	1	2	3	4
2. When I can be seen by customers, I am well groomed.	0	1	2	3	4
3. My work area is clean, neat, orderly, and safe.	0	1	2	3	4
4. Materials I give to customers are attractive, accurate, and understandable.	0	1	2	3	4
5. When speaking with customers, I use and pronounce words correctly and I use proper grammar.	0	1	2	3	4

Part 2. Action Plan

A. Tangibles Behavior	B. Steps to Achieve My Goal	C. Target Date	D. Completion Date
1. When I can be seen by customers, I am dressed neatly and appropriately.			
2. When I can be seen by customers, I am well groomed.			
3. My work area is clean, neat, orderly, and safe.			
4. Materials I give to customers are attractive, accurate, and understandable.			
5. When speaking with customers, I use and pronounce words correctly and I use proper grammar.			

Section IV. Empathy

Part 1. Self-Assessment					
Empathy Behavior	Never	Seldom	Sometimes	Usually	Always
1. When responding to customers, I stay calm and in control.	0	1	2	3	4
2. I acknowledge my customers' emotional states by using Empathy statements.	0	1	2	3	4
3. When a customer is upset, I find out what happened and work to bring things back to normal.	0	1	2	3	4
4. I am sensitive to individual customers' needs.	0	1	2	3	4
5. I am professional and caring at the same time.	0	1	2	3	4

This activity is available at: www.amacombooks.org:/go:/101ActDKYSOS
© 2009 AMACOM, a division of American Management Association.

Part 2. Action Plan

A. Empathy Behavior	B. Steps to Achieve My Goal	C. Target Date	D. Completion Date
1. When responding to customers, I stay calm and in control.			
2. I acknowledge my customers' emotional states by using Empathy statements.			
3. When a customer is upset, I find out what happened and work to bring things back to normal.			
4. I am sensitive to individual customer's needs.			
5. I am professional and caring at the same time.			

Section I. Responsiveness

Part 1. Self-Assessment					
Responsiveness Behavior	Never	Seldom	Sometimes	Usually	Always
1. I answer my phone by the third ring.	0	1	2	3	4
2. I acknowledge customers who are waiting for service.	0	1	2	3	4
3. I ask customers about their deadlines.	0	1	2	3	4
4. I greet customers with a smile on my face and in my voice.	0	1	2	3	4
5. I meet or exceed customers' standards for prompt service.	0	1	2	3	4

Part 2. Action Plan

A. Responsiveness Behavior	B. Steps to Achieve My Goal	C. Target Date	D. Completion Date
1. I answer my phone by the third ring.			
2. I acknowledge customers who are waiting for service.			
3. I ask customers about their deadlines.			
4. I greet customers with a smile on my face and in my voice.			
5. I meet or exceed customers' standards for prompt service.			

The Ten Deadly Sins of Service

Every customer has pet peeves—little things that annoy them beyond reason. *Knock Your Socks Off Service* is a positive, reaching-out philosophy. Part of serving well is also knowing what *not* to do. Following are ten "sins" you can avoid—behaviors and actions that some service providers exhibit that customers say annoy them most. These deadly sins align with the RATER factors, so have some fun with this!

PURPOSE:

✓   To learn what annoys customers most

✓   To match these to the RATER factors for a complete picture of customer perceptions

✓   To have some fun

TIME: 20 minutes

DIRECTIONS:

1. Prior to the meeting, photocopy the 10 "Deadly Sins" in Part A of Activity 25. Make a large chart, or write on a white board, the RATER factors (Reliability, Assurance, Tangibles, Empathy, Responsiveness).

2. Review the RATER factors with the group so they are familiar with them.

3. Explain that you are going to review the 10 sins, one at a time. As you do, they are to determine which RATER factor represents the opposite kind of service. (Note: You can also set this up in teams as a competition, with the first group to "buzz in" winning the point. If that team gets it wrong, the other team has a chance to guess. If you do a competition, be sure to have some prizes for the winning team—and maybe for the losers, too!)

4. Refer to Part B of Activity 25 for answers and explanations. You may choose to distribute the answers to the participants after the game is over.

5. Following the game, ask the group some of the following questions:
   - Did you recognize any of these "sins" as things you do?
   - What might you do to avoid committing this sin?
   - What is it about the behavior that irritates customers?
   - How might you recover the customer's goodwill if you commit a sin and realize it?

PART A

1. I don't know.

2. I don't care.

3. I can't be bothered.

4. I don't like you.

5. I know it all.

6. You don't know anything.

7. We don't want your kind here.

8. Don't come back.

9. I'm right and you're wrong.

10. Hurry up and wait.

PART B

1. "I don't know" relates to Assurance. One of the biggest reasons that customers often switch to Internet and catalog shopping is that sales staff don't know much about their stores' products and services. Certainly this ignorance undermines the ability to convey trust and confidence and to demonstrate knowledge and competence—factors that offer assurance to customers. Focus on product/service training so staff are better educated than customers.

2. "I don't care" relates to Tangibles. If you don't look or sound interested, or act as if you wish you were somewhere else, the customer will, too. Your appearance, posture, voice, focus, and attitude tell the story of whether or not you are proud of yourself and of the work you do. It doesn't take much for customers to pick up the message.

3. "I can't be bothered" relates to Reliability. If a personal phone call or conversation with a co-worker is more important than helping the customer, it says you're not willing to help and provide what is promised, dependably and accurately.

4. "I don't like you" relates to Empathy (also Responsiveness). If your behavior sends the message that "You're a nuisance, go away," customers will do just that. Take care in the tone of your voice, your body language, and how you focus on the individual.

5. "I know it all" relates to both Assurance and Empathy. If you jump in too fast or force a solution on the customer, that's being really pushy. Knowledge is a great tool to help your customers, but not a weapon with which to bludgeon them.

6. "You don't know anything" relates to Reliability and (over)Assurance. When you put down or demean a customer, you certainly are not providing what is promised, dependably and accurately. You goal is to help your customer. If you are rude to the person, you slam the door in his face and he will look for another door to walk through to get his business done.

7. "We don't want your kind here" relates to both Empathy and Responsiveness. This is flat-out prejudice, and it comes in all shapes and sizes, as do customers. Your job is to demonstrate care and concern for all customers and to be willing to help and provide prompt service. All customers deserve to be treated with dignity and respect. Your attitude shows in ways you may never even suspect.

8. "Don't come back" relates to Reliability. The purpose of serving customers well is to convince them to come back, again and again. When you do what is promised, consistently and predictably, the customer sees she can count on you. When you send the message that she's an inconvenience or you'd rather be doing something else, that sends the opposite message.

9. "I'm right and you're wrong" relates to Empathy and Responsiveness. What's the point of arguing with a customer? To prove something? Customers aren't always right, but it doesn't cost you anything to give them the benefit of the doubt. Be willing to help, and perhaps educate in a positive way, and you'll build a relationship with a customer who keeps coming back.

10. "Hurry up and wait" relates to Responsiveness. More than any other variable, time, or rather the lack of it, is the number one obsession of people today. Everyone is in a hurry. Demonstrate to the customer that you respect his time and are willing to help, and you'll find that he will respect you, too.

ACTIVITY 26

The Customer Is Always...
the Customer

The customer is not always right. You know it. We know it. And customers know it. Of course, customers should be given the benefit of the doubt in most situations, but to simply give in immediately and do whatever they ask is in many ways counterproductive. The-customer-is-always-right thinking can put a stop to real problem solving and customer education. Perhaps more dangerous is that the-customer-is-always-right thinking puts service providers in a one-down position. The goal of every service transaction is, and must be, to satisfy and delight customers in ways that will keep them coming back for more.

PURPOSE:

 To build on the concept that the customer is always... the customer

 To remind service providers how they set the tone in dealings with customers

TIME: 20 minutes

DIRECTIONS:

1. Ask participants to complete the phrase: "The customer is always... ."
    The typical response is "right." Quickly say, "No, you're wrong."
    Tell them that the correct answer is, "The customer is always...
    the customer!!"

2. Distribute copies of Part A Activity 26 and have participants complete or discuss the first part of the activity, Guilty Until Proven Innocent. Debrief the group by getting responses to the "How did you feel?" and "How did you act?" questions. Try to identify a pattern in the responses—it should be negative.

3. Have participants complete or discuss Part B of the activity, Receiving the Benefit of the Doubt. Debrief the group in the same way. The pattern should be better, if not positive!

4. Ask participants to discuss honestly how their customers are made to feel on a regular basis.

5. End with each participant stating one behavior they will change, or start or stop doing, to keep the focus on the customer a positive one.

PART A
Guilty Until Proven Innocent

1. Describe a situation in which a customer service professional treated you or someone you know as "guilty until proven innocent."

_____

_____

_____

2. How did you feel?

_____

_____

_____

3. How did you act?

_____

_____

_____

PART B
Receiving the Benefit of the Doubt

1. Describe a situation in which a customer service professional gave you or someone you know the benefit of the doubt.

   _____

   _____

   _____

2. How did you feel?

   _____

   _____

   _____

3. How did you act?

   _____

   _____

   _____

ACTIVITY **27**

Educating Your Customer

It's a principle of human learning that we remember best the things we discover for ourselves. So, rather than lecturing or blaming the customer, it is best to outline the situation and the facts, then let the customer draw his or her own conclusion—a process known as "educating through personal discovery."

PURPOSE:

✓ To learn by doing

✓ To appreciate the customer's perspective

✓ To experience the importance of being better educated than customers about products and services

TIME: 10-minute meeting, research, 30-minute meeting

DIRECTIONS:

1. When the group assembles, explain the purpose of this exercise. Tell them that the challenge is to see who is better informed— the customer or the service provider.

2. Have the group split into two teams, then explain how this activity works.

   • A product is selected for the two teams to research.

   • Team 1 goes out to businesses that sell the product to learn about it—features, benefits, costs, competitors, etc. Distribute copies of the first form from Activity 27 to the Team 1 participants.

- Team 2 researches on the Internet for information on the same product. This team does not speak to any service providers, but may visit blogs, customer review sites, and other sites to assist them. Distribute copies of the second form from Activity 27 to the Team 2 participants.

- There is no budget for this activity except regarding time. The time limit for discovery is 2 hours. (Hopefully, you can allow time during work or be able to pay for personal time spent.)

- Next week, the teams report on their research.

3. Select a product to be researched; for example, a GPS for the car, a high-end SLR digital camera, a Wii game system, a new business copier.

4. Set the teams loose to complete the activity.

5. When the group reassembles, ask the teams to report their findings.

6. Ask the group to determine which team gathered the most information versus the most *useful* information. Ask each team how much time it took them to complete the activity.

7. Ask Team 2 if they went to the same service providers as Team 1, but armed with the knowledge they acquired on the Internet, what *new* questions would they ask the service provider.

8. Discuss how this relates to the workplace. Remind participants that customers have more experience and access to more information than ever before. They are very well informed! Ask: how can participants be better prepared for their well-informed customers.

TEAM 1

1. What did I learn about the product from the customer service representative at the first location?

_____

_____

_____

_____

This activity is available at: www.amacombooks.org/go/101ActDKYSOS
© 2009 AMACOM, a division of American Management Association.

2. What did I learn about the product from the customer service representative at the second location?

_____

_____

_____

_____

TEAM 2

1. What did I learn about the product from the first Internet site I visited?

_____

_____

_____

_____

2. What did I learn about the product from the second Internet site I visited?

_____

_____

_____

_____

3. What did I learn from Internet blogs and customer review sites like Shopzilla, Amazon.com, or others?

_____

_____

_____

_____

ACTIVITY 28

Filling the Knowledge Gap

Customers frequently don't appreciate the time and effort that goes into the work service associates do for them. Your best bet for a successful interaction is to educate your customers about the work you do. With knowledge comes an appreciation of your efforts and expertise.

PURPOSE:

 To recognize when an education gap exists between customer and service associate

✔ To build a plan to educate the customer

✔ To reinforce "the customer is always… the customer" mind-set

TIME: 30 minutes

DIRECTIONS:

1. Remind participants that a critical part of their job is to educate their customers while at the same time making sure the customer feels like s/he is right. Three ways to do that are to:
   - Assume innocence
   - Look for teaching opportunities
   - Believe your customer

2. Distribute copies of Activity 28. With the whole group, list five common knowledge gaps your customers have regarding the products and services you offer. Ask participants to record these in column A.

3. Have participants form small groups. They will create "actions" to fill the knowledge gaps and write them down in column B. Ask for realistic target dates for completing these actions, and put these into column C.

4. With the whole group, discuss the suggestions that have been identi-fied. Build a plan to implement some of these "actions."

A. Customer Knowledge Gap	B. Actions You Will Take	C. Target Date for Competition
1.		
2.		
3.		
4.		
5.		

SECTION TWO

The How-To's of
Knock Your Socks Off Service

With the fundamentals of *Knock Your Socks Off Service* in hand, it's time to start putting those principles into action. The "how-to's" of service excellence are the behaviors used each day on the front lines to build customer trust and send the message that they're dealing with an organization that truly puts customer needs first and doesn't just talk about it in advertisements or marketing campaigns.

Whether it's serving customers in person, over the phone, via e-mail, or in instant Web chats, the tactical side of *Knock Your Socks Off Service* is about asking the right questions, quickly accessing the appropriate information, showing concern for customer needs, and adding a personal touch to service interactions that, all too often, have become formulaic or sterile. It's about learning to use both spoken and written words to communicate with clarity and empathy, wielding your headset or keyboard in ways that calm the turbulent waters of customer unrest.

It's also about knowing the strengths and weaknesses of the communication tools at your disposal. The true *Knock Your Socks Off* professional recognizes when customers are frustrated from endless e-mail or phone tag; it's recognizing when it's time to pick up the phone, soothe the nerves, and resolve a lingering problem. The *Knock Your Socks Off* professional understands that e-mail or instant chats, despite their many efficiencies, have limitations when it comes to communicating emotions or providing the personal touch that makes a difference— that keeps customers loyal to your organization.

As your customers grow ever more diverse, in terms of age, culture, race, or gender, *Knock Your Socks Off Service* also means acknowledging the differences among individuals and their distinct preferences for how they like to be served. Seeing your customers as individuals, not as stereotypes, is crucial to avoiding that kind of one-size-fits-all service approach that alienates customers and makes them feel like just another number or just another sale.

When they consider buying from you again, customers vividly recall how well they were treated the last time. Use the activities in this section to help your employees build a toolkit of skills that create passionate customers—customers who insist that all of their friends, family, and work associates also do business with you.

Good Question: Honesty

When it comes to customer service, honesty isn't just the best policy, it's the only policy. Lying to or misleading customers invariably leads to far worse problems than looking customers straight in the eye and telling them something unpleasant. Although truth-telling isn't always easy, service providers will find that customers respond better to honesty than to half-truths or attempts to sugarcoat a situation.

PURPOSE:

✓ To introduce the topic of honesty in a fun way

✓ To examine both sides of this topic

TIME: 25 minutes

DIRECTIONS:

1. Ask participants to think of a time when they told a "white lie" to a customer. You can use the following information to get the discussion going. Mention that, according to research done by Dr. John Tauer of the University of St. Thomas:

- 19 percent of us admit to lying in the workplace
- The top workplace lies are, "I don't know how that happened," "I have another call to take," "I didn't get your e-mail," "I like that _____/You look great."

- We lie because we have competing needs—being liked vs. being right and accurate.

- The need to be liked trumps the need for accuracy.

Have participants talk about situations in which they were tempted to tell a white lie.

2. Explain that there are two ways of looking at a white lie: there are times when telling a white lie is okay, or they are inexcusable under any circumstances. The group forms two teams. One team takes the position that it is okay to tell a white lie; the other team takes the opposite position.

3. Distribute copies of Activity 29 and give the teams 3 to 5 minutes to discuss their positions and jot down their points to support those positions. Remind participants they don't need to believe the position they are supporting, but they should form convincing arguments in support of that position.

4. Instruct the teams to listen closely and make notes as the other side presents its arguments. The idea is for one team to rebut the arguments of the other team. Give the first team 3 minutes to make the argument, then allow the opposing team 3 minutes to present counter-arguments.

5. Now give both teams 1 minute to formulate responses to the arguments just presented, followed by rebuttal arguments of 2 minutes per team.

6. Ask the group what conclusions can be drawn about being honest in the workplace. For example:

- What might customers conclude if they believe a company is lying to them?

- How much damage can even a "little white lie" do to a company's reputation?

- What is the impact of lying on customers' willingness to do business with you in the future?

- How might a lie impact a relationship with an internal customer?

ROUND 1
Declare and Support Your Position

Team Yes: "Of course, it's okay to lie when the situation warrants it."

Arguments: _____

_____

_____

_____

Team No: "No way, no where, no place, no how, no lies."

Arguments: _____

_____

_____

_____

ROUND 2
Rebuttal and Defense

Team Yes: _____

_____

_____

_____

Team No: _____

_____

_____

_____

Identify the Rules:
Red Rules/Blue Rules

We are so used to having rules in our lives that sometimes, when we don't know the answer or aren't comfortable making a decision on our own, we're tempted to make up a rule to fill the gap. Or, in the stress of the moment, we borrow a rule from another setting that seems to fit the current situation. It's important to understand the distinction between what we call "Red" rules and "Blue" rules when serving customers.

PURPOSE:

✓ To clarify the difference in types of rules

✓ To ensure that associates agree on organizational and departmental rules and recognize them as either Red or Blue.

✓ To establish the consequences for breaking a rule

TIME: 20 minutes (also works well in combination with Activity 31)

DIRECTIONS:

1. Distribute copies of Activity 30 to all participants and review the information differentiating Red rules and Blue rules. Be sure to have at least two examples for each rule type.

2. Ask participants to think about and jot down examples of the Red and Blue rules in both the organization and their department or area. Allow 3 to 5 minutes.

3. Solicit examples from participants, beginning with Red rules. As participants provide examples, this will naturally initiate discussion about whether or not other participants agree on the rule color. If there is disagreement, ask the question, "If I break this rule, will I be fired?" If the answer is yes, the rule is probably a Red one. If the answer is no or maybe, it is probably a Blue rule.

4. Solicit examples of Blue rules; the same type of discussion is likely to occur. Clarify whether rules are Red or Blue.

5. Discuss and define the different consequences of breaking Red and Blue rules.

Red Rules/Blue Rules

- **Red Rules.** These are rules that cannot be broken. They may be set by law or government regulation, or they may be in place to protect human life.

- **Blue Rules.** These are rules designed to keep operations running smoothly. They generally evolve out of department policy or past experience. Some Blue rules are borrowed from other situations, where they may be Red rules. You can bend or break a Blue rule in the name of improved service, since doing so won't cause harm or have irreversible consequences.

Do you know the Red rules and the Blue rules in your company?

1. List three of your organization's Red rules and give reasons for the rules.

    Rule 1: _____

    Reason: _____

    Rule 2: _____

    Reason: _____

    Rule 3: _____

    Reason: _____

2. List three of your organization's Blue rules and give reasons for the rules.

Rule 1: _____

Reason: _____

Rule 2: _____

Reason: _____

Rule 3: _____

Reason: _____

ACTIVITY **31**

Making Exceptions

Without formal and informal rules, service would become chaotic and customers would never know what to expect. If you believe an exception should be made to an existing rule, but aren't sure you can or should do it, ask a more experienced peer, your supervisor, or your manager. There are times when making exceptions to rules is justified in the name of meeting customer needs.

PURPOSE:

 To establish some guidelines for making exceptions

 To practice evaluating service situations and granting appropriate "favors" to meet customer needs

TIME: 20 minutes (consider pairing this with Activity 30 for greater impact)

DIRECTIONS:

1. Remind the participants that Blue rules can be bent or broken, depending on the situation. For example, a Blue rule in health care is that patients fill out admission forms before receiving any care. But in a unique situation, such as when a pregnant woman in labor arrives in the emergency room, this rule can be broken, with her admitted first and the forms filled out later.

2. Ask participants which rules are most often bent or broken for customers. Remind them to consider both external and internal customers. List these exceptions and discuss what exceptions are cited as reasons for bending or breaking these rules. List and discuss as you proceed.

3. Discuss how to determine when higher level permission is required to bend a rule and when associates may authorize an exception on their own.

4. Review Part A of Activity 31 and ask the following questions to identify special customers:

- Who would you say are special customers?
- How do you identify special customers?
- Are special customers *always* special customers?

5. With the participants, compile a list of who you consider to be your special customers.

6. Ask participants to pair up for a role-play. One member of each pair reviews a scenario in Part B of Activity 31 and presents the situation to the other. Then they switch roles for the next scenario.

7. Allow 3 to 4 minutes for each role-play scenario and 1 minute of feedback following each scenario.

8. Debrief the group on their experiences with the role-play activity by asking what went well and what did not.

PART **A**
Making Exceptions

If a rule is Blue, an exception may be considered. Knowing exactly when and how to make exceptions to Blue rules is easier said than done. You may choose to consider three types of exceptions:

- **The Little Favor.** Little favors are exceptions to Blue rules that are no big deal to you or the company, but that can mean a great deal to the customer. For example:

    CUSTOMER: I know the drug store doesn't open until 8:00 A.M., but since you're here, can I drop off this film?

    STORE EMPLOYEE: You are in luck! You've stopped by on just about the only morning I am ready enough to take your film.

- **The Big Favor.** When deciding whether to grant a big favor, consider three issues: (1) Will this exception cause too much delay in serving other customers? (2) Will it inconvenience another department in an unacceptable way? and (3) Is this a request you should pass along to a supervisor?

  CUSTOMER: I don't understand how I got an overdraft notice on my checking account. I deposited my paycheck Monday, but when I called the bank-by-phone line, they told me I have a negative balance.

  BANK EMPLOYEE: I can hear your frustration because of the overdraft notice. I think there may be some confusion. I'll send you a flier explaining our funds availability process. The money you deposited on Monday will be available to you tomorrow. In the meantime, I will make a special exception and reverse the overdraft charges and make sure no checks are returned for insufficient funds.

- **The Special Customer.** When you go to greater lengths for some customers than for others, you need to determine what the special customer was promised. You also need to determine who your most loyal and best customers are—those who have been with you the longest or contribute significant revenue to your bottom line—and determine how far you will go to serve these VIPs. For example, suppose Hupmobile is your number one client. So, you'd think, "They provide 75 percent of our revenue. Whatever they ask for, we will try to find a way to do it."

PART B
Role-Play Scenarios

Scenario 1. A customer calls to ask about an item in your inventory. The Web site shows that it is currently not available. Your research shows that the distribution center this customer uses is indeed out of stock, but the item is available from another distribution center. The cost of shipping will be more if the customer wants to use this option. Depending on the customer's history with your organization, choose one of the following Blue-rule exceptions:

- *Little favor.* You tell the customer the product is available from another shipping center and can be sent out the same day.

- *Big favor.* You tell the customer it is available and can be sent out the same day with no additional shipping charges because the distribution center was out of stock on the item.

- *Special customer.* You tell the customer it is available, can be sent out the same day, and you will waive any shipping charges to compensate for the inconvenience of being out of stock.

Scenario 2. A customer calls about an upcoming special celebration for his company. Tickets for the whole group to your local pro sports team are ordered. The group sales office handles these special requests. The customer is spending a fair amount of money and wonders what else you might offer him.

- *Little favor.* In addition to the deep discount on the ticket prices, you offer a block of special seats and the company's name on the Jumbo-Tron.

- *Big favor.* There is a deep discount on the ticket prices, special seating, food tickets for everyone attending (hotdogs, chips, and soda), and "Congratulations" on the Jumbo-Tron.

- *Special customer.* There are special seats for the group, even with a deep discount on ticket prices, food tickets for everyone, "Congratulations" on the Jumbo-Tron, and a meet-and-greet session with some of the players following the game.

ACTIVITY **32**

Why Customers Don't Trust

Trust is the platinum standard of customer service. The customer's faith in your word and belief in your promises are what saves you in those difficult times when everything else seems to be going wrong. Trust is particularly at risk when customers feel vulnerable, or when they perceive you hold all the power, and little or nothing is under their control.

PURPOSE:

✓ To recognize the value of building trust with customers

✓ To understand how a lack of trust can impact customer loyalty

✓ To connect customer trust with Assurance, one of the five RATER factors

TIME: 20 minutes (this activity leads nicely into Activity 33)

DIRECTIONS:

1. Make one photocopy of Part B of Activity 32 for your use as it includes the answers in parenthesis. Then photocopy the examples in Part B for each participant.

2. Distribute and review the information about trust in Part A of Activity 32. Discuss each reason that customers will lack trust: freedom, information, expertise, recourse.

3. Distribute Part B and ask participants to review the first row of examples and determine which trust factor is missing. Allow 2 to 3 minutes.

4. Discuss their answers. If they provide incorrect responses, help them analyze the situations and move them to the correct conclusions.

5. Move to the second set of examples and repeat the process. Allow only 2 minutes for their work.

6. Ask participants for examples of when they have experienced a customer who was lacking trust. Have them describe the situation and offer reasons for their conclusions. Ask what trust factors may have been missing for the customers in those situations, or what past experiences made them wary of the organization.

7. Review the RATER factors (Activities 5, 6, and 24). Remind the participants of the connection between trust and the Assurance factor.

8. Briefly discuss how participants can reduce or eliminate the lack of trust for their customers. And, most important, provide steps they can take to increase the customers' level of trust.

PART **A**

Customers don't trust when they lack the following:

- *Information.* They don't know what is going on, or how long it will take to set things right.

- *Expertise.* The customer couldn't fix his car or computer, or fouled up the online reservation he made. All the "smarts" are on your side of the table.

- *Freedom.* There is no option for fixing the problem aside from dealing with you. The customer perceives you as the only hope.

- *Recourse.* The customer perceives that, when it comes to this computer or car or malady, it's you or nobody. The customer may be free, contractually, to ask anyone else to fix the problem, but there is no one else, or at least the customer sees it that way.

PART B

Examples of Lack of Trust			
"I realize you're new to the area, and I realize you need to see your personal physician in order to get the tests you need, but we're unable to take any new patients for at least 2 weeks." (freedom)	"Both of these HDTVs look to be about the same according to the specs provided on these cards. I really can't make any recommendations for you." (expertise)	"I've got a call in to my supplier, but he's not calling me back. I really couldn't tell you when your wedding ring will be in." (information)	"Look, my car has been here at the dealership for 3 days! You told me it would be finished 2 days ago! What is going on?" (recourse)
"My flight has been canceled and I have to get to Dallas tonight for a very important meeting tomorrow—please, isn't there some way you can help me?" (expertise)	"After pulling up your file, Ma'am, I don't see any record of that deposit. You'll have to call again tomorrow to see if it's gone through." (information)	"This is so frustrating! You should've told me I couldn't get coverage in my area with this phone. Why can't you let me out of my contract?" (recourse)	"I prefer cable over satellite TV; you're the only cable provider, so will you match their special prices?" (freedom)

ACTIVITY **33**

Create an Environment of Trust

Trust builds slowly, over time and through a series of positive experiences. But there are some things you can do to speed the building of trust in your dealings with both customers and co-workers.

PURPOSE:

✓ To generate a list of behaviors and actions that support a trusting environment

✓ To emphasize service personnel as a vital link in the trust-building chain

TIME: 20 minutes

DIRECTIONS:

1. Ask participants to form small groups of three to five individuals each.

2. Distribute copies of Activity 33.

3. Ask groups to discuss the following topics and keep notes. Allow 5 to 8 minutes.

   • Why is it important to create an environment of trust?

   • What is trust?

   • What behaviors support an environment of trust? (For example, "keeping promises to customers or co-workers.")

   • What specific actions can individuals take to build an environment of trust?

4. Ask each group to present the results of its discussion. Allow 2 to 3 minutes.

5. Because the groups have more notes on paper than they are likely to present in the time period, ask a volunteer to gather the pages, then compile them and distribute to the group as a reminder of the specific actions each person can take to create an environment of trust.

Create An Environmnet of Trust

Discuss the following topics:

* Why is it important to create an environment of trust?

* What is trust?

* What behaviors support an environment of trust? (For example, "keeping promises to customers or co-workers.")

* What specific actions can individuals take to build an environment of trust?

Behaviors that Support Trust	Specific Actions that Support Trust

Barriers to Effective Listening

Most of us pay attention to only about 25 percent of what we hear. We tune out the other 75 percent—in one ear and out the other, as if we've never heard it. Yet being a good listener, and hearing what your customer is saying, is a critical skill. There are a number of obstacles we must surmount on the road to better listening.

PURPOSE:

✓ To recognize the many barriers to good listening ability

✓ To consider the impact that poor listening skills has on customer perceptions and loyalty

✓ To build a plan that eliminates or minimizes participants' most prevalent barriers to good listening

✓ To practice good listening behaviors

TIME: 20 minutes (this activity is also effective when paired with Activities 35 to 38)

DIRECTIONS:

1. Distribute copies of Part A of Activity 34 to the participants.

2. There are a number of effective ways to review the barriers to good listening. The facilitator may present them, providing examples of each. Or a large group discussion can cover the subject, with everyone contributing examples. Or small groups can discuss the types of barriers and report back to the whole group with their examples.

3. Once the review is complete, ask participants to identify a barrier they know is a particular problem for them. Distribute copies of Part B of Activity 34 and have participants complete the form individually.

4. Explain to participants that, now that they have thought about their personal barriers, they have an opportunity to practice eliminating them. Ask participants to select partners and then have the pairs discuss their most challenging barriers. The activity calls for one partner to use a listening barrier to distract the other, to experience the frustration of poor listening. Spend 2 to 3 minutes. Have the pairs repeat their conversations with their partners, this time demonstrating effective listening skills. Allow another 2 to 3 minutes.

5. Have the pairs reverse roles, again demonstrating, first, poor listening skills and, then, good listening skills. Again, allow 2 to 3 minutes per session.

6. Use the following questions to discuss the problems inherent to poor listening behavior:

- What was your reaction when your partner didn't appear to be listening to what you said?
- Similarly, how might customers pick up on your inattention to what they are saying?
- What can you do to overcome your own inattention and listen better to what a customer is saying?

7. Ask participants to use Part C to make a personal commitment to improve listening.

PART A

Think of some examples of how these barriers block your ability to listen effectively.

1. External noise

   Examples: _____

   _____

2. Interruptions

   Examples: _____

   _____

3. Mental detours (daydreaming, thinking of the next question you want to ask or the response you will give, wondering when the customer will get to the point, etc.)

   Examples: _____

   _____

4. Technology

   Examples: _____

   _____

5. Stereotypes of customers

   Examples: _____

   _____

6. Trigger words and phrases

   Examples: _____

   _____

7. Attitude

   Examples: _____

   _____

PART B

Select one of the barriers you identified in Part A.

Barrier: _____

1. How does this barrier affect you? _____

    _____

    _____

    _____

2. How does it affect your relationship with your customers? _____

    _____

    _____

    _____

3. How can you overcome this barrier? _____

    _____

    _____

    _____

PART C

Select one of the barriers you identified in Part A that is particularly challenging for you. Set a personal goal to improve your listening skills by eliminating this most challenging barrier.

My Goal: _____

_____

_____

_____

Go Ahead, I'm Listening

It's never too late to start improving, because good listening skills, like any other skill, get better with regular practice. Just prove it! Let me know you're listening.

PURPOSE:

✓ To practice the skills of active listening

✓ To experience the difference when someone really listens to what you are saying versus when they are just going through the motions

TIME: 30 minutes

DIRECTIONS:

1. Explain to participants that this exercise will help them improve their active listening skills. Distribute and review copies of Part A of Activity 35 on paraphrasing, summarizing, and repeating back information. (Note: It might be helpful to quickly demonstrate the skills for the participants.)

2. Ask participants to form groups of three, if possible, or pairs if the number of participants won't allow for this.

3. Distribute copies of Part B of the activity. Explain the rules of the activity:

   • One person is designated the speaker; the other the listener; if working in three's, the third is the observer. Speaker and listener are to engage in a conversation.

- The speaker picks a topic and begins to talk.
- The listener listens to the speaker but cannot ask a question of the speaker unless he or she first uses one of the active listening skills.
- If there is no observer, the speaker pays attention to the listener to see if a listening skill is applied before asking a question. If there is an observer, that person stops the listener if the rule has not been applied and reminds the listener to paraphrase, summarize, or repeat back before asking a question.

- Give the participants 4 to 5 minutes for the first conversation.
- Immediately following the conversation, the speaker provides feedback to the listener on his or her demonstration of active listening skills.
- Remind participants that this exercise may feel awkward because the skills will be exaggerated, but to continue nonetheless.
- After there's feedback on round one, have the pairs/trios switch roles and repeat the process. Conduct a round three if there is an observer, this time with the observer taking the speaker's role.

4. Debrief by asking the following questions:
- How hard or easy was this activity?
- What worked and what didn't work?
- As a listener, what did you learn about the other person?
- As a speaker, what did it feel like to have someone listening so attentively?

5. Distribute copies of Part C and ask participants to commit to really listening to their customers for the next week, using the active listening skills just practiced. Ask them to use the form in the activity to note what they learned from listening to customer responses, changes in the length of their conversations, and improvements in their listening skills.

PART A
Good Listening Skills

- *Paraphrasing:* repeating what the speaker is saying in your own words

- *Summarizing:* recapping in your own words what has been said in a conversation, using fewer words

- *Repeating back:* restating the exact words the speaker has used

PART B
Engage in a Conversation

Speaker Role. Select one of these topics to discuss:

- What might be a dream vacation for you?

- What home improvement project have you been putting off?

- What do you particularly like about working at the company, or in your department?

- What is your personal strength or weakness?

- What do you do for fun and relaxation?

Listener Role. Engage in a conversation with your speaker based on the topic the speaker introduces. When you want to ask the speaker a question, first use one of the skills (paraphrasing, summarizing, repeating back) to confirm what s/he has said.

Observer Role (optional). When the listener begins to ask the speaker a question, stop the listener if s/he does not first paraphrase, summarize, or repeat back what the speaker has said. Be prepared to offer a suggestion to help the listener.

This activity is available at: www.amacombooks.org/go/101ActDKYSOS
© 2009 AMACOM, a division of American Management Association.

PART C
Listening to Customers

My commitment to improved listening for the next 7 days:

What I learned	
What my customers' responses were	
How the length of my conversations changed	
How my skills improved during the past 7 days	
What do I still need to work on?	

This activity is available at: www.amacombooks.org/go/101ActDKYSOS
© 2009 AMACOM, a division of American Management Association.

Follow My Lead

A good dialogue requires both great listening and great questioning skills. Indeed, it's hard to be a good questioner without first being a good listener, so it's important to master both skills in your interactions with customers.

PURPOSE:

✓ To practice good listening and good questioning skills

✓ To recognize the value of a give-and-take dialogue

✓ To have some fun

TIME: 20 minutes

DIRECTIONS:

1. You will need the following materials for this activity: a handout of the diagram for Activity 36 and seven playing cards for each team. (Note: There will be one extra card per team.)

2. Challenge participants to use their very best listening skills while not asking any questions. Review the value of good listening.

3. Ask participants to find a partner, then determine who will be the listener and who will be the speaker.

4. Explain the activity:

- Each speaker receives a copy of the diagram on page 128. The speakers should conceal the diagram from the listeners.

- Each listener receives seven playing cards (it doesn't matter which seven) and puts them face down on the table.

- Each pair is to sit back-to-back so the speakers cannot see the listeners and vice versa.

- The listeners attempt to match the pattern on the diagram by arranging the cards on the table as directed by the speakers. Other than the directions being given by the speaker, there should be no noise, no questions, no grunts or groans, no prodding, no laughing—in short, no feedback whatsoever.

- The pairs have 3 minutes to arrange the cards.

5. Call time and have the groups check the card arrangement to see how well it corresponds with the diagram. Solicit feedback on the activity.

6. If time allows, run the activity again. This time, allow questions and feedback but continue to prevent participant pairs from seeing one another.

7. Ask participants how many got the placement right the second time, when questions were allowed.

8. Ask participants what they have learned. Look for responses like, "It's really important to listen," "It's hard when no feedback is allowed" (a crucial factor in good dialogue), "Even when there is a flowing dialogue, people often don't communicate clearly or don't listen well," "I can appreciate how customers get frustrated when good listening or questioning skills aren't used in conversation."

ACTIVITY 37

Listening: Taking a Mental Detour

The most common of all listening "sins" is taking a "mental detour" (see Activity 34). Most of us are guilty of letting our minds wander when we're speaking with customers. With our focus on the speaker slipping, we start to ponder our next question, where we're going to lunch, or what indelicate thing our spouse or friend said earlier that day. It's tough to mask inattentive listening; most customers know when you've taken a mental detour. So it's important to work on giving clients our undivided attention.

PURPOSE:

✓ To recognize how easy it is for our minds to wander during conversations

✓ To create strategies for overcoming this barrier to good listening

TIME: 20 minutes

DIRECTIONS:

1. Distribute copies of Activity 37 to all participants. Define the "mental detour" and describe it as perhaps the biggest barrier to good listening. Provide examples for better understanding.

2. Allow 5 minutes for participants to estimate the percent of time they take mental detours with different people and identify what steps they will take to minimize this barrier.

3. Solicit ideas from participants for other ways to avoid mental detours.

4. Suggest that participants keep the activity sheet posted in the workplace as a reminder to continually work on improving their concentration and to verify that estimated percentages are accurate.

Listening

If a customer or co-worker is speaking to you at the rate of 150 words per minute (the average), and you forget to listen for even 15 seconds, you've missed 37 words of the message. Tune out for 30 seconds, and 75 words have flown past you without ever registering. Is it any wonder that mental detours lead to so many misunderstandings and mistakes?

1. Estimate what percentage of the time you tune out when listening to the following people:

Customers   _____

Co-workers   _____

Your supervisor   _____

Your best friend   _____

Your spouse/significant other   _____

Your children   _____

2. List two steps you will take to minimize your mental detours.

1. _____

   _____

   _____

2. _____

   _____

   _____

Crafting the Best Questions

To be successful with the unsure or unclear or confused customer, you need to put on your detective hat. And, like Sherlock Holmes, Columbo, or the criminalists on *CSI*, you have to go in search of clues. Armed with a supply of good questions, you are sure to succeed.

PURPOSE:

✓ To script questions for use in a variety of situations

✓ To practice writing and asking questions

✓ To become more consistent in gathering good information

TIME: 30 minutes

DIRECTIONS:

1. Distribute copies of Part A of Activity 38 and review with participants the three types of questions suggested for customer inquiry: Background, Probing, and Confirmation questions.

2. Ask participants to form small groups of two or three people each. Give them copies of the scripting sheet found in Part B of the activity.

3. Explain that the purpose of this activity is to help participants recognize the value of scripting questions in advance. Explain that scripting gives them a variety of questions they can readily access; it is not about reading questions verbatim, as if from a script. This exercise is designed to build confidence and consistency in dealing with customers.

4. Ask participants to write at least two questions for each category.

5. Have each group read their questions aloud. As each is read, ask the others to consider what information will be gleaned from the customer's response. Be sure that probing questions are open-ended. If not, as a large group work to rewrite the question.

6. As a conclusion, ask for a volunteer to gather the pages and create a master copy for distribution to all participants so questions are available for future customer contacts.

7. Challenge participants to use these questions over the next two weeks and tell them to be prepared to report back on their application, customer response, and usefulness.

PART A

Customers are often less than articulate about their wants and needs. To be successful with the unsure or unclear or confused customer, you need to put on your detective hat. Use three types of questions with your customers to search for clues.

1. *Background questions.* These questions are the introduction to your conversation. They tell you who you are talking with and help you evaluate whether you are the best person to help the customer. These are typically close-ended questions. For example:

   • Do you have an account with us?

   • May I have your customer identification number as it appears just above the label on the back of the catalog?

2. *Probing questions.* These questions help you delve more deeply into a customer need, problem, or complaint to identify the issues involved and begin to move toward a solution. Probing questions are usually open-ended. A good source of probing questions is the basic five W's: Who? What? When? Where? and Why? For example:

   • Tell me more about your event: who will be attending, what they will be expecting, and how last year's event could be improved upon?

   • What features are you looking for in a new bike?

3. *Confirmation questions.* These questions help you confirm that you've correctly understood the customer's message; they give the customer an

This activity is available at: www.amacombooks.org/go/101ActDKYSOS
© 2009 AMACOM, a division of American Management Association.

opportunity to add information or clarification. These are most often close-ended questions, but may be either closed or open. For example:

- That takes us through the aftercare regime Dr. Kling prescribed. The exercises are the most important part and they can be challenging. Would you like to review them again?

- So, if we could provide you with a partial order today, enough product to see you through Monday, will that solve your immediate problem?

PART B

Now it's your turn. Script two unique questions for each of the question types that focus on dealing with customers.

Background Questions

1. _____
   _____

2. _____
   _____

Probing Questions

1. _____
   _____

2. _____
   _____

Confirmation Questions

1. _____
   _____

2. _____
   _____

ACTIVITY **39**

The Name Game

"Only when you begin to ask the right questions do you begin to find the right answers," says Dorothy Leeds in the book, *Smart Questions: A New Strategy for Successful Managers.* There are many types of questions you can ask to better understand customer wants and needs. Each type of question will solicit different types of information, so it's important to know how and when to use each type for maximum effectiveness.

PURPOSE:

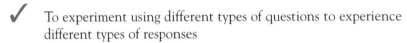

✓ To experiment using different types of questions to experience different types of responses

✓ To understand what types of questions work best in various service scenarios

TIME: 20 minutes

DIRECTIONS:

1. Prior to the meeting, copy and cut out each name in Activity 39. Place each name in an envelope. Give an envelope to each participant, and direct participants not to open the envelope or look at what is inside.

2. Divide participants into pairs. Direct pairs to open their partner's envelope and place the name on the partner's back, without letting the partner see the name. The activity will be for the partners to ask questions of one another in an attempt to discover the names on their backs. The names are those of people well known to most of us. Emphasize that participants can use any type of question that they like during the exercise; the only question they cannot use is "Who is the

person on my back?" Direct participants to keep track of the number of questions they need to ask before discovering the name. Begin the activity by directing one person in each pair to ask the first question.

3. After one person in each pair has discovered the name, direct the pairs to switch roles and then the other person asks the questions to discover the name on his or her back. Allow up to 3 minutes for each partner's turn.

4. Debrief by asking the following questions to highlight key learning points.

- What did you know about the name before you even began to ask questions? (The name was of a well-known person.)
- How many questions did you ask before you discovered the name on your back?
- What are some examples of questions you began with?
- How did the nature of your questions change as you proceeded to gain information?
- How did you use close-ended questions in the exercise? What types of answers or outcomes did those questions produce?
- How did you use open-ended questions? What types of answers or outcomes did they produce?
- How will this exercise help you ask better questions when dealing with customers?

LeBron James	Abraham Lincoln
Osama Bin Laden	Chris Rock

Regis Philbin

Oprah Winfrey

Mario Lopez

Sarah Palin

John McCain

Tim Russert

Barack Obama

Barbra Streisand

Nancy Pelosi

Billy Graham

Madonna

Mother Theresa

Prince William

Derek Jeter

Muhammad Ali

Angelina Jolie

Tiger Woods

Paula Abdul

Steve Carrell

Kelly Clarkson

ACTIVITY **40**

Who Knows?

Customers are often less than articulate or even clear in their own minds about their wants and needs. Probing, open-ended questions help you pinpoint the problem or identify the confusion involved and move toward a solution. Open-ended questions generally require more lengthy explanations and invite customers to join in conversation.

PURPOSE:

✓ To learn the value of asking open-ended questions

✓ To formulate questions as open-ended

✓ To experience the customer's perspective

TIME: 30 minutes

DIRECTIONS:

1. Review with participants the three types of questions, especially probing, open-ended questions.

2. Ask participants to form groups of three each—the number is important for this activity. One member of the trio serves in the role of customer; another is the service provider; and the third is an observer. Participants rotate through each role, in turn. Explain that the purpose of the activity is to practice using open-ended questions.

3. Participants work through each scenario, rotating roles each time. The role of the customer is just that. The role of the service provider is to uncover the customer's problem. The role of the observer is to make

sure the service provider uses open-ended questions and follows the rules.

4. Explain the rules to participants:

- The customer initiates the role-play.

- The service provider must always ask an open-ended question in order to move forward or ask any other questions.

- The observer stops the action if the service provider doesn't ask open-ended questions; the observer challenges the service provider to rephrase the question.

- The goal is not to solve the customer's problem but to gather as much information from the customer as possible.

- The time limit is 5 minutes for each round—4 minutes in the role-play, followed by 1 minute for feedback to the service provider.

5. Distribute copies of Activity 40 and begin the first role-play. Keep track of time and keep the rotation going.

6. Debrief by asking the following questions:

- What was the most challenging aspect of this activity?

- What did the service provider discover about the customer?

- How did the activity change as the role-play continued?

- In what situations do you think open-ended questions are most valuable?

ROUND 1

- **Service Provider.** You are a cable and high-speed Internet service provider. A customer is on the phone and seems confused about some problem or need. Your job is to find out what the problem is and direct the customer to the correct department. If the problem is wireless Internet service, the correct department is you. Remember to ask good open-ended questions.

- **Customer.** You are calling your cable and high-speed Internet provider because your Internet service is down. Initially you are confused about whether it is the Internet or the cable service that is causing the problem. You think that these services use the same cable. You don't have a clue how it all works and are confused by technology. If the service provider asks you an open-ended question, give a little bit of information at a time. You goal is to have the service provider send someone out who can fix the problem and explain the whole system to you.

- **Observer.** Read both the service provider and customer roles. Be sure to listen for and manage the use of open-ended questions. Before the service provider can ask a close-ended question, be sure that an open-ended question has been asked first. If that does not happen, stop the role-play and have the service provider rephrase the question to be open-ended. If help is needed, please provide some.

ROUND 2 (Rotate the roles.)

- **Service Provider.** You are a manufacturing company providing personalized labels for many different products—for tee-shirts, caps, inside clothing labels, on jackets, or on any other accessory item. You have a customer on the line who is new to your company and is calling to gather information about your products, pricing, and services. The customer really has no idea what she wants and the call seems like a waste of your time. Although you want to be polite, you would like to get the customer off the phone to help the "real" customers. Remember to ask good open-ended questions.

- **Customer.** You are calling a manufacturing company that provides personalized labels. This is the first time you are looking for this type of product, so you need to gather a lot of information. There could be any variety of items that will need to be personalized, from hats, jackets, and tee-shirts to folios, awards, and more. You could potentially be spending hundreds of thousands of dollars, as the purchase is for a huge conference your company is sponsoring. But you give out only a little bit of information at a time. Your goal is to have the service provider send you a proposal for personalizing a variety of items at a quantity of 5,000 for three items, 1,000 for one item, and 10 for one item.

- **Observer.** Read both the service provider and customer roles. Be sure to listen for and manage the use of open-ended questions. Before the service provider can ask a close-ended question, be sure an open-ended question is asked first. If that does not happen, stop the role-play and have the service provider rephrase the question. If help is needed, please provide some.

ROUND 3 (Rotate the roles once more.)

- **Service Provider.** You are a health-care provider in your city. Your advertising says that, regardless of whether or not a person carries your insurance, you will help them find a doctor near them. When you answer the phone, you get a person who is new to the city and is gathering information about health care, service providers, and types of benefits. You decide to send the individual some information to review and then answer questions based on that. This person doesn't want to hang up and keeps posing different situations for you to respond to. Remember to ask good open-ended questions.

- **Customer.** You are new to the community and need to gather information about various health-care providers. As a distributor, you need to secure your own insurance. The company you represent offers an allowance for insurance if the insurance company meets several criteria. The provider must offer a full range of services—doctors, hospital, urgent care, maternity, etc. It also must offer various levels of deductibles and pharmacy coverage. As you are new in town, you aren't sure where the facilities are or what communities the providers serve. You do want information mailed to you, but you would like to gather as much information as possible over the phone because you need to make a decision quickly. You are hesitant about giving out too much information at a time. Your goal is to have the service provider give you complete information so you can compare the offerings of different companies.

- **Observer.** Read both the service provider and customer roles. Be sure to listen for and manage the use of open-ended questions. Before the service provider can ask a close-ended question, be sure an open-ended question is asked first. If that does not happen, stop the role-play and have the service provider rephrase the question. If help is needed, please provide some.

ACTIVITY **41**

How Did I Do?

After a big game, sports teams often review tapes of their performance. They analyze, dissect, and discuss each play. Such "after action" reviews are a great way to learn what you are doing right—and wrong. It's all about improvement. While it's not always easy to listen to our own voices on tape, reviewing and analyzing our phone interactions with customers after the fact is one of the best ways to learn about good and bad conversation habits. (Note: This activity is specifically for call-center employees and their supervisors.)

PURPOSE:

✓ To identify individual strengths and weaknesses in questioning skills

✓ To discuss ways to change or improve performance

✓ To listen to service transactions from the customer's perspective

✓ To build a stronger employee-supervisor relationship

TIME: 20 minutes (depending on the length of the call), conducted one-on-one with supervisor and employee

DIRECTIONS:

1. If your call system allows, pull a recent sample or two from the employee's interactions with customers. Give employees copies of the Call Review Sheet (Activity 41) and a place to quietly listen to and review their calls. (Note: This may be done together if the employee is comfortable doing so. If not, have the employee listen privately, then conduct the review together. [It is likely you will be replaying and listening to the calls together.])

2. Plan two to three areas for change/improvement. Set a time to meet again to listen for the proposed changes in the employee's service approach or behavior. This should be at least 2 to 3 weeks out.

Call Review Sheet	
What types of questions did I use in this interaction? (Background, Probing, Confirmation)	
Did I use both open-ended and close-ended questions?	
Were the probing questions all open-ended?	
When using open-ended questions, did I get more helpful information from my customer?	
What was my customer's reaction to the questions I asked? What did I hear in the customer's tone of voice that is a clue to his/her reaction?	
How might I rephrase a question to get a more desired response?	

ACTIVITY **42**

When Questions Go Wrong

The right question that is poorly timed or badly worded can undo all of the customer service magic you've worked so hard to create. Remember to put yourself in the customers' shoes when you start to "interrogate" them.

PURPOSE:

✓ To learn when and how to ask appropriate questions

✓ To discover the impact of a poorly timed or badly worded question

TIME: 20 minutes

DIRECTIONS:

1. Distribute copies of Parts A and B of Activity 42. Review the four times when questions go wrong, referring to the handout.

2. Ask participants to read the brief scenarios that describe when questions go wrong and rewrite them in a way that makes the questions more inviting for you and your customer.

3. Debrief by soliciting the rewritten responses to the scenarios. Ask participants, "What type of reaction might this situation solicit from the customer?" referring to the reasons questions go wrong, not to the scenarios themselves.

4. Ask participants to think of a time when they got a surprise response from a customer and had to backtrack or explain the reason for the question(s).

PART **A**

There are four times when questions go wrong.

1. The question is asked at the wrong time, possibly out of sequence. There is logic to the order in which questions should be asked.

2. The customer thinks you are asking about something he believes you should already know. Explain that you are verifying some required information.

3. The customer feels you are asking too many questions. Make your questions count, for you and for your customer.

4. The questions feel too personal. What's personal and what's just conversation varies from person to person. If you're asking because you're curious, it may be better not to; if you're asking because you need the information, use the preview technique to explain why the information is necessary—before you ask the question.

PART **B**

Read the brief scenarios below and rewrite each one to ask questions in a more appropriate way.

Scenario 1: "Thank you again for calling. It was really a pleasure talking with you and I look forward to working with you on this project. What was your name again?"

Your rewrite: _____

_____

_____

_____

Scenario 2: "Oh, hi, Marcus! It's great to hear from you! How was your vacation? Did the kids have a great time? Well, it's nice to have you back. I'll be sure and have Lucy call you back as soon as she gets back in. If you could just spell your last name and give me your phone number that would be great!"

Your rewrite: _____

_____

_____

_____

Scenario 3: "Hello, ma'am. Are you the lady of the house? How are you today? Are you enjoying the warm sunshine? I just have a couple of questions for you. Do you have some time to talk to me?"

Your rewrite: _____

_____

_____

_____

Scenario 4: "Okay, we just need to get a few details out of the way and we can get you registered. What is your annual income? And the income of your spouse? Oh, wow! Do you make any alimony payments? And how much is that each month? What is your Social Security number? And then finally, I need your credit card number. And what's the name on the card? Expiration date? Thank you so much, now we can go ahead and process your application."

Your rewrite: _____

_____

_____

_____

ACTIVITY **43**

Winning Words and Soothing Phrases

We are capable of bruising or soothing our customers with words; it all depends on how we use them. Some words, alone or in combination, create immediate negative images. It's not the intent of your words to cause customer anger but it is sometimes the effect. The goal of a *Knock Your Socks Off* professional is to avoid or defuse the emotions that words might cause.

PURPOSE:

✓ To create awareness of the "Forbidden Phrases"

✓ To change wording from negative to positive

✓ To recognize individual opportunities to improve

TIME: 30 minutes

DIRECTIONS:

1. Remind participants that we all have "trigger words" that cause us some anger or ire. Point out that there are recognized Forbidden Phrases in the service world.

2. Advise participants that this activity is to create awareness of those Forbidden Phrases and change the intent of statements from potentially negative to positive.

3. Hand out copies of Part A of Activity 43 and read the examples. Ask participants to work with one or two others to rewrite the Forbidden Phrases so that they become positive Winning Words. Allow 7 to 8 minutes for this. (Note: The answers are found in Part B.)

4. When time is up, discuss with the group each Forbidden Phrase and listen to the revisions that participants have written. If there is a phrase that doesn't seem to be positive, first ask the group how they would respond when hearing those words, then help them to rework the example to be more positive.

5. After completing the worksheet, ask participants to pick one or two of the phrases that they can work on for the next week. It is often a good idea to work with a partner who can listen or observe, triggering an alert lest participants fall back into old behaviors. Ask participants to pick a partner to work with on this.

Note: Back on the job, many departments have fun with this. Examples of how they have used the activity include creating a "No Problem" jar; for each infraction—someone who uses a Forbidden Phrase—he or she must deposit a quarter in the jar—the proceeds are then used for a celebration. A variation on this is to use a "flag" on a stick to alert someone when s/he is heard using a Forbidden Phrase (it's waved to point out the infraction); another approach is to create a "traveling" award for the associate showing the greatest improvement in eliminating Forbidden Phrases, with associates selecting a winner each week.

PART A

Forbidden Phrases	Winning Words
"I don't know."	
"We can't do that."	
"You'll have to…"	
"Hang on a second; I'll be right back."	

Continued

"No," when used at the beginning of any sentence.	
"No problem." "Not a problem." "No worries."	
"Honey" or "Lady" or "Hey, pal" or "Buddy"	
"Our policy/procedure is…"	
"The system won't allow for that."	
"It's over there" (and point).	

PART B

Suggested Positive Responses

Forbidden Phrases	Winning Words
"I don't know."	"That's a good question. Let me check and find out."
"We can't do that."	"Let me suggest what I can do for you"; "Here's what I can do for you…"
"You'll have to…"	"I might suggest…"; "I'll ask you to…"; "The next time that happens here's what you can do…"
"Hang on a second; I'll be right back."	"It may take me a couple of minutes. Are you able to hold while I check?"; "May I put you on hold while I check?"

Continued

"No," when used at the beginning of any sentence.	Eliminate the "no" and say the sentence; change the negative to a positive—"I'm happy to replace the product as I'm not able to refund your money."
"No problem." "Not a problem." "No worries."	If asked to do something, "Certainly" "I'll be happy to"; "It's my pleasure" If someone says thank you, say "You're welcome"
"Honey" or "Lady" or "Hey, pal" or "Buddy"	The customer's name (the way s/he wishes it to be used)
"Our policy/procedure is…"	If you can make an exception once, "I am able to make an exception this time. In the future, please be aware…"
"The system won't allow for that."	"At this time, I am able to manually make that request"; "Our system is currently set up to…"
"It's over there" (and point).	"Let me walk you over there." Or, "Do you see the blue sign? It's just to the left of that."

Scripting Better Responses

Service people are often reluctant to use scripts, for fear they will sound robotic or mechanical in their interactions with customers. And that can happen. But service scripts can work effectively as guidelines when (1) they are short and easy to remember; (2) they are developed around situations that are important to customers; (3) people are free to put the thoughts into their own words so they don't sound forced or mechanical.

PURPOSE:

✓ To create positive responses to nagging problems

✓ To build consistency in associate responses

✓ To practice the scripts to create a change in behavior

TIME: 30 minutes

DIRECTIONS:

1. Remind participants that there are common problems, questions, and situations customers will present, to which they will need to respond, many times per day or week. Ask participants to help create a list of what these problems and questions are. List them on a chart paper or white board.

2. Explain that the goal of this activity is to build consistency in how the group responds to these pesky issues. You will do that by scripting some positive responses.

3. Distribute copies of Activity 44 and review the examples. Ask the participants if these sound scripted. When you script a response, the sentence should sound natural and positive.

4. Using the examples as a guide, ask participants to pair up and select one of the problems on your list. Ask the pairs to script a positive, customer-friendly response.

5. Debrief by having each pair read its script.

6. Ask for a volunteer to collect and prepare the scripts for distribution to the group. Ask participants to try these scripts during the next week and to keep notes on how well the scripts worked for developing their customer responses.

7. OPTIONAL: Create quick scenarios that reflect typical customer concerns, so participants can test the scripts as they would sound in real situations.

Some Examples

1. Patient surveys conducted at Baptist Health Group in Pensacola, Florida, told employees that a sense of privacy was important for most patients. So nurses scripted a statement designed to acknowledge and reinforce that expectation: "I'm closing this curtain to help protect your privacy." Almost immediately, patients started rating nurses, doctors, and med techs higher on their thoughtfulness and consideration.

2. Travelers visiting the Peabody Hotel in Little Rock, Arkansas, often engage in pleasant conversations with the hotel doorman, who delights in asking them: "Can we expect you back at the Peabody?" When being assured of a repeat visit, he closes this chapter of the conversation with the scripted: "Then we'll look forward to seeing you again very soon."

Scripting

Select one issue from the list of problems and situations you created as a group. Create a script for use in resolving that problem in a positive, customer-friendly manner.

_____

_____

_____

_____

_____

_____

_____

_____

_____

_____

_____

ACTIVITY 45

Give a Nonverbal Cue!

What is nonverbal communication? It's everything we don't say. It's our body language, how we act and react—and what we show to others when we are with them. *Knock Your Socks Off Service* professionals are keenly aware of the different types of nonverbal communication and their impact on customers.

PURPOSE:

✓ To create awareness of types of nonverbal communication

✓ To identify the positive and negative impacts of nonverbal communication on customers

✓ To have fun while learning

TIME: 20 minutes

DIRECTIONS:

1. Distribute copies of Activity 45 and review with the group the nine dimensions of nonverbal communication.

2. Ask the group to pair up, and then act out each situation described, identifying both a positive and a negative impact of each nonverbal cue. An example for eye contact might be: positive impact is that making regular eye contact sends a message you are listening; negative impact is that you send a message what the speaker is saying isn't important.

3. Debrief by asking what observations the pairs made and what they learned by doing this exercise.

4. Ask participants to identify atypical nonverbal behaviors—those that aren't demonstrated through physical movements. (For example, the appearance of daydreaming, attention to background noise, giving signs of not feeling well, or being distracted.)

5. Ask participants to commit to change, improve, or eliminate one of their nonverbal behaviors that could be having a negative impact on customers.

Nonverbal Cues

1. *Proximity.* This refers to physical distance from the other person. Begin a conversation while standing about an arm's-length apart. After a few minutes, move forward until your noses are about 6 inches apart. What is your acceptable bubble of personal space?

   • Positive impact _____

   • Negative impact _____

2. *Eye contact.* Looking directly at a person while you speak or listen implies you are paying attention. Continue the conversation with your partner while making eye contact. Now change it to make no eye contact—look away as you speak. What amount of eye contact is comfortable for you?

   • Positive impact _____

   • Negative impact _____

3. *Silence.* You can and do communicate even when you are saying nothing. Remain silent while your partner is talking, providing nonverbal cues such as head nodding when necessary to show agreement or smiling when you choose to. How does silence affect the conversation?

   • Positive impact _____

   • Negative impact _____

4. *Gestures.* Closed gestures, such as tightly crossed arms, hands tucked deep in pockets, or clenched fists, imply resistance and are nonverbal barriers to communication. Open gestures invite people into our space and say that we're comfortable with what they are saying. Many of our gestures are unconscious (some people cross their arms when the room is cold, for example). How do gestures impact conversation and customer perception?

   • Positive impact _____

   • Negative impact _____

5. *Posture.* "Stand up straight," your mother always said, and she was right. Good physical posture conveys confidence and competence. Leaning in slightly when customers are talking says you think what they are saying is important and interesting. Experiment with various posture positions with your partner.

   • Positive impact _____

   • Negative impact _____

6. *Facial expression.* A raised eyebrow communicates surprise; a wink indicates sly agreement or alliance; tightly set lips, opposition; a wide open smile, friendliness. Your face communicates, even when your voice doesn't. Use different expressions with your partner and observe the reactions you get.

   • Positive impact _____

   • Negative impact _____

7. *Physical contact.* What is and is not appropriate today varies greatly with the situation, the part of the world you're in, and the people involved. A handshake is customary, but placing a hand on another person's arm or an arm over someone's shoulder can be a personal act. Practice your handshake and professional greetings with your partner. What is important to communicate in your handshake?

   • Positive impact _____

   • Negative impact _____

8. *Smell.* This is an important nonverbal in service work that involves getting close to customers. Be just as careful with strong perfumes and colognes—some customers may be sensitive or allergic—as you are of the natural odors they are used to cover up. Be aware, too, that at a time when fewer adults smoke, the lingering smell of tobacco can be offensive. Identify the scents around you and determine if they have a positive or negative impact.

   • Positive impact _____

   • Negative impact _____

9. *Overall appearance.* Just as in a theatrical performance, you have to look your part. Whether your costume is a three-piece suit or blue coveralls depends on the job you do, what you want to communicate to customers, and especially what your customers expect to see. Work with your partner to identify the positive and negative attributes about your appearance today.

   • Positive impact _____

   • Negative impact _____

Face-to-Face Charades

The words we speak, hear, or read are only a small part of the way we communicate with one another. Experts suggest that, in face-to-face situations, at least 70 percent of what is communicated is done without speaking a word. How well do you pick up on the cues that signify meaning? This exercise is a form of the game of Charades with a twist.

PURPOSE:

✓ To get participants quickly familiar with verbal and nonverbal cues

✓ To consider customers' reactions to verbal and nonverbal responses

TIME: 30 minutes

DIRECTIONS:

1. Prior to the meeting, photocopy and cut out the flash cards for Activity 46 (Part A).

2. As a large group, briefly review Part B of Activity 46, on verbal and nonverbal cues.

3. Explain to participants that the game is a great, fun way to become more familiar with the different verbal and nonverbal cues—signals —that people give through their behavior.

4. Participants select a flash card and then each "acts out" his or her verbal or nonverbal cue as a negative service behavior. The observers guess what the cue is, based on the handout sheet (Part B) listing the negative behaviors.

5. When a correct guess is offered, the participant who is "acting" suggests one reaction a customer may give to this cue. The rest of the group may also offer suggestions.

6. When all cues have been used, discuss as a group which of these behaviors may be most offensive to customers. (The real answer is all of them!) Ask participants to reverse the behaviors and describe how the opposite cue sends a positive message. (For example, negative-behavior eye contact is to either not make any eye contact or to stare at a customer; positive-behavior eye contact is to make initial eye contact and then give as much eye contact as you get from the customer.)

7. Ask participants to commit to using only positive nonverbal communications with customers and to observe the difference in reactions they receive from their customers as a result.

PART **A**
Flash Cards

Eye Contact	**Proximity**
Negative eye contact is to give none at all— don't look at the customer, or stare at her without blinking.	Negative proximity is to invade the personal space of customers. Stand within 12 inches of the person.

Voice Pitch

End every sentence by having your voice go up in pitch, as if asking a question. This diminishes customer confidence.

Check Watch or Clock Frequently

This negative nonverbal behavior sends a message that the customer is not as important as something else you have to do.

Voice Tone

Using a monotone voice—all one pitch—tells customers that they aren't important and perhaps even boring.

Eye Movement

By either rolling your eyes or having your eyes dart about the room, you send a message that you aren't focused on customers and their issues aren't important.

Mumbling

Unclear speech—mumbling, using too many "um's," improper enunciation, or emphasis on the wrong words—tells customers you lack confidence.

Touch

Touching, hugging, or patting someone's back is not acceptable in the workplace. Customers will be put off by this behavior.

Facial Expressions

Out-of-context facial expressions—
smiling at something sad, surprise when
asked a question—confuse customers
and derail the conversation.

Accents

A heavy accent provides an opportunity
for customers to make assumptions
about you—correct or incorrect.
Listening also is more difficult when
a thick accent is present.

Daydreaming

Heading off on mental detours sends
a message to customers that their
concerns aren't important.

Trigger Words

Certain words or phrases can cause a
smoldering fire to burst into flame—in
both your customer and you (examples:
lazy, stupid, detached; phrases like
"I assumed you would have known
that"). Because we can never be
sure what words trigger customers, it's
important to use positive or neutral
language whenever possible.

Gesturing

Flailing hands, constant motion,
tapping fingers, or other gestures can
be distracting and confusing. Gestures
also can be interpreted differently
depending on culture. What is seen as
positive or neutral in your country might
be deemed offensive in another.

Vocal Pacing

Talking too fast or too slow can
cause confusion and frustration in
service situations.

Appearance
How you physically present yourself, and your work area, influences customer perceptions of you and the company and their willingness to keep doing business with you.

Distractions
Talking on a cellphone or to an associate, or clicking away at a keyboard while on the phone, detracts from your professional service image and send the message that the customer isn't a high priority.

PART B
Verbal and Nonverbal Cues

1. **Verbal Cues**

   - Vocal quality: tone of voice, pacing, articulation, accent, intonation, energy level

   - Trigger words or phrases

2. **Nonverbal Cues**

   - Proximity

   - Eye contact

   - Silence

   - Gestures

   - Posture

   - Facial expression

   - Physical contact

   - Mental detours

   - Distractions

   - Appearance

ACTIVITY **47**

Receiving Nonverbal Cues

The flip side of giving nonverbal cues is receiving the cues your customers give you. Service-savvy professionals train themselves to read nonverbal communications and act according to the signals they see.

PURPOSE:

✓ To practice interpreting nonverbal messages

✓ To modify personal behavior based on the cues we receive

✓ To discuss situations in which it's difficult to decipher customer cues

TIME: 20 minutes (this exercise works well in combination with Activity 46)

DIRECTIONS:

1. Remind participants of the range of nonverbal behaviors they may observe in customers. (See Activities 45 or 46.)

2. Ask participants to form either pairs or small groups, and then to review the two situations in Part A of Activity 47. They should identify both the nonverbal cues being made and the appropriate responses to them. Allow 5 to 7 minutes.

3. Debrief by reviewing their responses to the activity. Talk through any differences in interpretation. See Part B of Activity 47 for examples.

4. Ask participants to think of (both internal and external) customer interactions during which they may have been confused by a customer's response or have observed a dramatic change in a customer's behavior. Use the following questions as prompts:

- Briefly describe the situation.
- What specific behavior or change did you observe?
- What reaction did that cause in you?
- How did you handle the situation after the change in behavior?

PART A
Situations

- **Situation 1.** You are meeting with an internal customer in her office. At the beginning, the meeting is relaxed and cordial. The co-worker greets you with a smile, and uses expansive gestures when inviting you to sit down. She has maintained good eye contact, nodded and smiled in agreement, and leaned slightly forward as you reviewed the status of your project. But as the conversation continues there are subtle shifts in her body language. Her facial expression has become tense and her speech becomes more rapid. She also has started wringing her hands and looking at her watch. She's pushed her chair back from her desk slightly, briefly summarizes your discussion, and asks, "Is there anything else we need to discuss right now?"

  A. What has your customer told you nonverbally?

  _____

  _____

  B. What might explain the change in her behavior?

  _____

  _____

  C. How will you respond to the change in the customer's signals?

  _____

  _____

- **Situation 2.** You are a customer service representative for a credit card company. Mr. Green has phoned to accept a mail invitation that indicates he has been preselected to apply for a credit card at a low introductory interest rate. He also wants to transfer a balance from another credit card. You are taking his application over the phone. Initially, Mr. Green was friendly and enthusiastic about the offer. He provided his Social Security number, date of birth, address, and phone number without hesitation. Now, as you move into the more sensitive questions about income, house payments, and employment, the customer sounds somewhat nervous. He begins to clear his throat and hems and haws about answering questions. He challenges, "Why do I have to answer these questions? Your offer says I'm preselected. I just want to get my credit card and arrange the balance transfer."

   A. What has the customer told you through his vocal signals?

   _____

   _____

   B. What could explain the change in the customer?

   _____

   _____

   C. How will you respond to the customer?

   _____

   _____

PART B
Responses

Situation 1

   A. For most of the meeting, the customer's nonverbal signals said, "Welcome. Have a seat. I'm glad we're having this meeting. I'm very interested in working on this. I like your ideas." Then the customer started feeling some heavy-duty time pressure, exhibited by the glances at her watch, hand wringing, and faster speaking rate. Her nonverbal signal that the meeting was over occurred when she pushed her chair back from her desk, just before she asked if there was anything else you needed to discuss.

B.   There may be many reasons for the change in behavior. She may have another meeting scheduled; she may need to leave; she may have heard something in what you said that caused her to feel pressured or confused about roles and responsibilities; she may have to use the bathroom.

C.   Your communications strategy now is to wrap things up as quickly as you can. Follow up the meeting with a memo or e-mail summarizing your discussion and listing any actions agreed to with target dates.

Situation 2

A.   At the beginning of the conversation, the customer's vocal signals indicate openness, eagerness, and cooperativeness. When the line of questioning turns to income and employment, the customer becomes nervous, closed, and defensive.

B.   The customer's motivation in phoning rather than mailing the application could be eagerness to accept the offer, a dislike of the paperwork associated with filling out the form, or both. Initially the customer was comfortable giving the customer service rep personal information. Then something changed and the customer became nervous and guarded. If the service rep neglected to explain to the customer why he was asking questions about income, the customer could have felt the questions were unnecessarily personal—a classic case of a question gone wrong. The customer may have misunderstood the language of the credit card offer. Since he was "preselected," he may have thought he was exempt from providing financial information. If the customer was between jobs or having financial or domestic problems, he might have been worried about his eligibility for the card.

C.   The service rep's first response should be to use an Empathy statement and explain why the company needs this information even though the customer has been preselected for the card. If the customer agrees, the service rep can continue with the application. If the customer is unwilling or unable to provide the information, the rep can explain how to proceed once the customer has the necessary information.

ACTIVITY **48**

Telephone Checklist

Being a *Knock Your Socks Off Service* provider on the phone requires a lot of skill, patience, and practice. Customers cannot hear your facial expressions or see such nonverbal clues as shrugs or hand gestures. But they do form a mental picture of you based on the tone and quality of your voice.

PURPOSE:

 To compare perceived performance with actual performance

 To heighten awareness of important behaviors for telephone service

TIME: 10 minutes (this may be combined with Activity 49 for follow-up and skill practice)

DIRECTIONS:

1. If your department is a call center or participants spend a significant amount of time on the phone with customers, this checklist will be very helpful. Have a short discussion with participants about the significance of service phone skills.

2. Make two copies of the Telephone Checklist (Activity 48) for each participant.

3. Distribute the checklists and ask participants to complete the first assessment alone and to answer the statements based on how well they think they do when assisting customers over the phone.

4. Direct participants to use the second copy of the checklist at their desks and complete it right after finishing a call. Ask them to compare their initial (perceived) responses against the responses based on an actual call.

5. Ask participants to be prepared to answer the following questions:
   - How closely did your estimated responses match the real thing?
   - What might you need to do more of, stop doing, or change as a result of this comparison?

Telephone Checklist

Note: You might want to make extra copies of the checklist and keep them handy so participants can check their phone skills every so often to look for changes or improvements in behavior.

		Yes	No
1.	Promptness of Answer	____ Rings	
2.	Greeting		
	Did you use a salutation?	____	____
	Did you use a clear and appropriate identification statement?	____	____
	Did you ask how you could help?	____	____
	Did your tone establish rapport?	____	____
3.	Was the call transferred to you?	____	____
	If yes, how many times was the caller transferred?	____ Times	
	Were you able to help the caller during this call?	____	____
4.	Did you transfer the call?	____	____
	If yes, did you preview the transfer process (let the customer know why he was being transferred)?	____	____

Did you offer the name and number that you were transferring to?　　＿＿＿　＿＿＿

Did you "walk" the caller through the transfer (staying on the line until it was successfully completed)?　　＿＿＿　＿＿＿

5.　Did you take a message?　　＿＿＿　＿＿＿

Did you gather complete information (i.e., the caller's name, company name, phone number, other relevant data)?　　＿＿＿　＿＿＿

Did you confirm the spelling and the phone number with the caller?　　＿＿＿　＿＿＿

6.　Did you place the caller on hold?　　＿＿＿　＿＿＿

Was a hold appropriate for the situation?　　＿＿＿　＿＿＿

Did you ask the customer's permission?　　＿＿＿　＿＿＿

Did you check back regularly (every 30 seconds)?　　＿＿＿　＿＿＿

Did you thank the customer for holding?　　＿＿＿　＿＿＿

7.　Were you able to answer the caller's questions quickly?　　＿＿＿　＿＿＿

If necessary, did you refer the caller to the proper person or department?　　＿＿＿　＿＿＿

Did you ensure the customer received a satisfactory response to his question or problem?　　＿＿＿　＿＿＿

8.　Did you make the customer feel that you knew what you were doing?　　＿＿＿　＿＿＿

9.　Were you courteous and respectful?　　＿＿＿　＿＿＿

ACTIVITY **49**

Be a Standout on the Phone

Many times service professionals never meet their customers in person, so the customer remains "just a voice on the phone." But that doesn't give you permission to be distant and anonymous. Telephone relationships can be just as personal and successful as face-to-face relationships.

PURPOSE:

✓ To build some standardization at critical points during telephone communication

✓ To create agreement among associates concerning outstanding phone skills

✓ To heighten awareness of phone etiquette

TIME: 20 minutes

DIRECTIONS:

1. Distribute copies of Part A of Activity 49. Remind participants of the critical points in telephone communication by looking together at the handout: greeting, putting a caller on hold, transferring calls, apologizing for any delays in service, and more. Ask participants to work together to list the qualities and standards in the appropriate boxes that help make the department a world-class phone service provider. Allow 10 minutes. (Note: Part B offers suggested responses.)

2. Review the group's responses, box by box. If there is not an agreed-on set of standards for each action, this is a great time to create one. For example, a wonderful, easy, and consistent greeting might be, "Hi, ABC Billing Department. This is Andrew. How may I help you?" (Note: When you get to the voice mail box, be sure to explore both the delivering and receiving aspects of each individual's voice mail greeting and how to leave a proper voice mail message for someone else.)

3. Once the phone service standards are established for the group, ask for a volunteer to compile them, duplicate them and distribute copies to the group. Determine a time frame for implementation and follow-up.

PART A
Phone Situations

Using the phone to do your job requires you to be more aware of your voice than in other situations. The tone, pace, and quality of your voice has a big impact on customer satisfaction with a phone interaction. In addition, your mood, be it smiling and happy or tight-lipped and angry, comes through loud and clear to customers when you are on the phone. List the qualities below that will make you a standout phone service provider.

Greeting	Putting a Caller on Hold

Call Transfers	Taking a Message
Voice Mail Messages	Closing the Call

PART **B**
Suggested Responses

Greeting "Hi, ABC Billing Department. This is Andrew. How may I help you?" Another option is to say, good morning or afternoon. Note: If you are talking to people all over the U.S. or world, this may not be as good an option. You want to offer some form of a greeting, identification statement, and suggestion of assistance.	**Putting a Caller on Hold** "Are you able to hold while I look that up?" or "May I put you on hold while I access that information?" The key is asking the customer for permission; and waiting for a response. The customer may prefer to have you call back. Involve the customer!
Call Transfers Your goal should be to do everything within your power to help the customer yourself. No one likes to be transferred and repeat the same information two or three times to different people. If you must transfer, provide the customer with the name and phone number of the person to whom you are transferring the call in case there is a problem making the connection.	**Taking a Message** Be sure to get the caller's full name, company, and phone number. If a customer is reluctant to provide that, a great statement is, "For quick reference, may I have your name, company, and best number to reach you?"

Voice Mail Messages

Your own: If you plan to be away from your desk for more than two hours, let callers know so they can anticipate some delay in a return call.

Leaving a message. Leave your name and number twice—once at the beginning of the call and once at the end. As you say your number, speak slowly, pretending you are writing it down just as the person receiving the message will have to do.

Closing the Call

Ask if there is anything further you can help with. Do say "thank you" to the caller, even if he is calling with a complaint! Soliciting possible complaints at this stage at least gives you an opportunity to try to fix them. Customers who experience problems, but aren't asked by the company if they had any, are more likely to silently walk away disgruntled and start doing business with your competition.

ACTIVITY **50**

Just Phone Home!

Because the phone is such an integral part of all business operations, it's critical that we present our best service selves when using that communications vehicle. What does your voice sound like? How do your associates answer the phone—really? What do customers hear in the background? How are transfers really made in your department? How good is your company's phone technology at meeting customer needs, rather than just being cost-effective?

PURPOSE:

✓ To hear what you really sound like on the phone

✓ To test the effectiveness of your phone system for meeting customer needs

✓ To experience phone etiquette from the customer's perspective

TIME: Two meetings, one 5 minutes, another 20 minutes

DIRECTIONS:

1. Explain to participants that we never reach the finish line with phone skills—there is always an opportunity to improve.

2. Tell participants that they will take time out of their workday to experience the company's phone service through the customers' eyes. Distribute copies of Activity 50 and ask that they:

   • Call their own voice mail and listen to the message.

   • Call the main line for the company and ask to be directed to a particular department or, if they reach a voice mail menu, to enter the number that will connect them to a live service rep.

- Call their department and speak with the representative who takes the call.
- Call their department's voice mail system directly and attempt to reach a live person.
- Record their experiences on the phone logs below.

3. At the follow-up meeting, ask participants about their telephone experiences. Listen for tales of consistency or inconsistency, of satisfaction or frustration. Ask them what surprised them about these experiences as customers.

4. Solicit suggestions for changes or improvements to the system based on their phone experiences. Make a plan to incorporate one or more of these suggestions by a specific date.

CALL 1
To Your Voice Mail

Date: _____   Time: _____

1. How did your own voice message sound?

   _____

2. How inviting was your greeting?

   _____

3. Are customers offered an option to leave a voice mail message?

   _____

4. Is there a request to leave a detailed message?

   _____

5. What background noise did you hear?

   _____

6. What else did you learn by calling your own message?

   _____

This activity is available at: www.amacombooks.org/go/101ActDKYSOS
© 2009 AMACOM, a division of American Management Association.

CALL 2
To the Company's Main Line for Incoming Calls

(You ask to be transferred to a department)

Date: _____   Time: _____   Area called: _____

1. Did the first person you talked to do everything possible to help you before transferring your call?

   _____

2. Did the initial contact brief the person who received the transferred call so that you didn't have to repeat your information?

   _____

3. Was the person you were transferred to there to take your call?

   _____

4. If not, were you able to leave a detailed message?

   _____

5. Was the person you were transferred to able to assist you?

   _____

CALL 3
To Your Department

Date: _____   Time: _____   Area called: _____

1. How did the voice of the person who answered sound?

   _____

2. How inviting was her or his greeting?

   _____

3. Were you offered an option to use voice mail if the person was not available?

   _____

4. Were you able to follow the prompts and directions that were provided?

   _____

5. What background noise did you hear?

   _____

6. When you asked to be transferred, what did you hear during the transfer?

   _____

7. What else did you learn?

   _____

CALL 4
To Your Department's Voice Mail

Date: _____   Time: _____   Area called: _____

1. How many options did you have to listen to prior to hearing the one for your situation?

   _____

2. Were the options clearly stated and was one appropriate for your situation?

   _____

3. Was there an option to connect to a person immediately?

   _____

4. What did you hear during the transfer?

   _____

5. What problems and shortcomings did you experience with the department's voice-mail system?

   _____

This activity is available at: www.amacombooks.org/go/101ActDKYSOS
© 2009 AMACOM, a division of American Management Association.

Telephone Etiquette: Secret Shopper

Your customer is on the phone. How efficiently or cheerfully you meet her needs can make the difference between keeping her as a loyal customer or watching her defect to the competition. Observing how other organizations provide customer service over the phone—what they do right and what they do wrong—is a good way to improve your own phone skills.

PURPOSE:

✓ To observe other organizations' attention to phone service quality

✓ To involve participants in learning from these observations

✓ To apply these lessons to your own organization

TIME: Two meetings, one 10 minutes, one 20 minutes; observation time varies (consider pairing this with Activity 50 for greater impact)

DIRECTIONS:

1. Review what qualities make for stand-out customer service over the phone.

2. Explain to participants that one great way to learn what others are doing well to demonstrate outstanding telephone skills is to take on the role of secret shopper. Explain that this is the goal of the next several days—to observe how other service providers interact over the phone.

3. Ask participants to define the role of a secret shopper (see earlier activities), then how they might function in that role for this activity. Listen for responses like, "Ask more challenging questions or to be transferred to another department," "Call multiple times to compare skill levels of more than one person," "Make notes about what other organizations do to demonstrate outstanding telephone skills," "Call multiple locations in the same organization to check for consistency," "Make unusual or strange requests to see how they are handled."

4. Ask participants to pick two organizations they will contact in the next week. Distribute Part A of Activity 51 and have them prepare up to three questions to ask the selected businesses. During these interactions, they will be secret shoppers. Distribute copies of Part B of Activity 51 and ask them to keep detailed notes of the telephone service skills they experience.

5. At the follow-up meeting, ask participants to share their observations, both positive and negative. Keep a list of both on separate chart papers or other recording devices.

6. Review the list of negative points and remind everyone that these behaviors are what you want to avoid!

7. Review the list of positives and ask the group how these telephone skills might be incorporated into the work they do or used to reinforce habits that are already in place. Ask each person to commit to making one change in behavior and adding one skill to their skill set.

Part A

What three questions will I ask the person I talk with?

1. _____

   _____

2. _____

   _____

3. _____

   _____

PART B

Call Log			
	Who Did I Contact?	What Did They Do Well?	What Do They Need to Work On?	How Will I Incorporate What I Learned into My Own Behavior?
Contact 1				
Contact 2				

ACTIVITY 52

Tongue Twisters with a Twist

Using the telephone requires that you be more aware of your voice than at any other time. That's why it's important to regularly exercise and "tune up" your vocal and facial muscles, just as you would other muscles in your body. Tongue twisters can serve as good calisthenics before you start a service shift.

PURPOSE:

✓ To get your vocal and facial muscles loosened up to work smoothly

✓ To practice proper pronunciation

✓ To learn tongue twisters that also have a service message

TIME: 10 minutes (This is a great ice-breaker for any meeting.)

DIRECTIONS:

1. When the participants assemble, explain the purpose of this activity.

2. Distribute copies of Activity 52, or write the tongue twisters on a flip chart or white board.

3. Ask the group to say the tongue twisters slowly, then gradually increase the speed.

Note: For an added degree of difficulty, don't allow participants to read the tongue twisters beforehand.

TONGUE TWISTERS

- Service Superstars Save Sales

- Be E.T.D.B.W.—Easy To Do Business With

- Customers are service-centered and service-sensitive

- Your walk talks. Your talk talks. But your walk talks louder than your talk talks

- A noisy noise annoys a customer

- Please pay promptly

- Probing problems prompts progress

- Strange strategic statistics

- Six sticky sucker sticks

- A big black bear bit a big black bug

- Aluminum linoleum

- Unique New York

ACTIVITY **53**

E-Mail vs. Telephone

Service professionals spend an increasing amount of time interacting with customers through e-mail as well as on the phone. Although e-mail or instant chats can be an efficient way to handle some customer matters, there are times when using the phone remains the best path to customer satisfaction. How do you know when to use each communication tool to ensure the best experience for customers?

PURPOSE:

✓ To build organizational guidelines for when to use e-mail or telephone

✓ To clarify how different communication methods impact customers

✓ To remind participants that internal and external customers have communication preferences

TIME: 30 minutes

DIRECTIONS:

1. Ask participants to form small groups of three to five people each and provide each group with the scenarios in Part A of Activity 53. Each group will need to decide whether to use e-mail or the phone to address the matter at hand. Allow 5 minutes for the groups to discuss each scenario. An answer sheet for facilitators is in Part B of the activity.

2. Review with whole group the strengths and weaknesses of both e-mail and phone communications, as shown in Part C of Activity 53.

3. Ask the group to provide examples of experiences, both as service provider and as customer, of when either e-mail or the phone was better for handling service issues.

4. Remind participants that different generations often have different communication preferences. For example, some older people (Veterans and Baby Boomers) might prefer interacting using the phone to discuss a problem, while younger generations (GenXers and Millennials) often prefer e-mail or instant chats. Use the following questions to begin a discussion:

   • What are your own communications preferences? For example, do you prefer to have problems addressed by someone on the phone or via e-mail?

   • In dealing with your customers, what have you noticed about generational preferences?

5. In small groups again, have participants create guidelines for determining when to use e-mail or phone in your department. With the entire group reassembled, have each individual group report on these guidelines and use them to create a master list for using e-mail and phone contacts that will have the greatest impact on customer satisfaction levels. Ask for a volunteer to prepare and distribute the guidelines to participants.

PART A
Scenarios

• **Scenario 1.** A 60-something customer finds what he believes to be a bank error in his online banking statement. After a number of back and forth e-mail messages with customer service reps to identify the source of the problem, the two sides remain at a stalemate, unable to solve the problem. The customer's frustration level is growing. At this point, what communications channel is the most effective way to satisfy this customer?

• **Scenario 2.** A customer who speaks English as a second language phones your call center seeking advice on how to use the features of his new Global Positioning Satellite (GPS) system. Because of his awkwardness using English, he has a hard time understanding your directions. He ends the conversation by saying he now has the answers he needs, but you are certain he hasn't understood what you've said. What communications method is best for working with this customer to achieve real satisfaction?

- **Scenario 3.** A customer is having trouble making his new financial software application function correctly, and sends an urgent e-mail to your customer call center. The center responds by having a service representative engage the customer in an instant chat session. After 20 minutes of text suggestions from the rep, the customer still isn't able to get the software working properly. What communications method is best for continuing to work with this customer?

- **Scenario 4.** When you get a break at work, you see that you have a voice-mail message on your cellphone. You listen: "Hi, Shane, this is Liz at Houses Today. I just heard back from the seller's agent that we didn't get the house. Sorry. Call me." What is the best communications method for Liz in working with this customer?

PART B
Suggested Answers

- **Scenario 1.** Given the customer's age, state of agitation, and the extent of e-mail back and forth, communicating via phone now is the best option. It allows the bank rep to convey more emotion in an apology—regardless of who is at fault—and put a human face on the organization, thereby resolving the problem and keeping the customer satisfied.

- **Scenario 2.** When your customer is still learning English, a phone conversation may not be as clearly understood as the written word. Sending an e-mail with instructions, or offering a link to your Web site's FAQ, may be a better option, since it allows the customer to print out and study the instructions. The bottom line is that it is often easier to read a new language than it is to understand it spoken. It's your call, but often both methods should be used. Try the phone, then follow up with an e-mail.

- **Scenario 3.** With problem resolution going nowhere, it is more effective to ask that the customer phone the call center, where representatives can employ a hybrid solution. When the customer calls in, a service rep can use a screen-sharing tool that enables the rep to view the customer's computer screen as he uses the application, talking him through the changes and helping to locate the source of the problem. Without this combination of voice and online support, there might be an endless trail of e-mail or instant chats before the issue is resolved.

- **Scenario 4.** When you have to deliver bad news, it's best to make a human connection—use the phone. Your customer may want you to use e-mail, text messaging, or leave a voice-mail message, but we recommend a live conversation. You may choose to leave a voice-mail or e-mail message to have the customer contact you.

PART C
The Comparitive

<table>
<tr><td colspan="2" align="center">Strengths and Weaknesses of Using E-Mail</td></tr>
<tr><td align="center">Strengths</td><td align="center">Weaknesses</td></tr>
<tr><td>Ability to provide thoughtful, detailed responses</td><td>Difficulty in communicating emotion or providing a personal touch</td></tr>
<tr><td>Creates a valuable paper trail</td><td>More back and forth with customers, since incoming customer e-mails don't always have all the details necessary to troubleshoot problems</td></tr>
<tr><td rowspan="2">Round-the-clock access by customers or service reps</td><td>Need for high-level writing skills</td></tr>
<tr><td>Inability to respond to extremely time-sensitive requests (such as making changes to an imminent flight departure)</td></tr>
</table>

Strengths and Weakness of Using the Telephone

Strengths	Weaknesses
Improved ability to convey caring and empathy	Need to think faster on your feet, responding on the spot to customer questions or problems
Better context for interactions (the spoken word is harder to misinterpret)	Greater challenge remaining calm in the face of irate customers
More effective for complex interactions that involve a lot of exchange between customers and service providers	Higher communications costs
Ability to resolve more customer issues or problems on first contact	Communicating across different time zones can be difficult

Strengths and Weakness of Using Instant Message or Online Chat

Strengths	Weaknesses
May function much like a "real" conversation	Not as personal as a live conversation
Can work through questions or problems quickly	May misinterpret the context of the question
Technology familiar to many users	May take a bit longer due to slow typing skills of both customer and service provider
	Frequently includes jargon or acronyms that customers don't recognize, causing more questions

ACTIVITY **54**

Written Communication Review

Why are you writing to your customer? Because you have something to say and a reason to say it. There are three main reasons for using written communications in the workplace. We write to: (1) confirm understanding; (2) create documentation; and (3) solidify a relationship.

PURPOSE:

✓ To view written communications and e-mails from the customer's perspective

✓ To heighten awareness of the written communications that come from your organization

TIME: 20 minutes (This activity may tie in with Activities 14, 15, and 62.)

DIRECTIONS:

1. In preparation for this activity, ask participants to collect two or three pieces of printed material they have received at home from companies they do business with or who have solicited their business.

2. At the meeting, ask participants to "show and tell" the materials they brought in. Ask participants which category the examples fit:
   - Confirm understanding
   - Create documentation
   - Solidify a relationship

3. Follow up by asking the participants what impact these printed pieces had on them as customers. Remind them to keep the above responses in mind. OPTIONAL: If you have worked on the RATER factors, remind participants that these written materials are Tangibles.

4. Brainstorm with the group all the ways that the written word is used in your organization that directly impact your customers. Look for answers like: "advertising," "Web site copy," "marketing materials," "coupons," "contracts," "orders," "billing," "manuals," "annual reports," "pamphlets," "instructions," "enclosures," "e-mails," "e-blasts," "faxes," "letters." List these on chart pad and post for all to see.

5. Create three separate chart pads, and label and post them as follows:
   • Confirm understanding
   • Create documentation
   • Solidify a relationship

6. Have participants place the types of written communications they listed (from the first chart pad) in one of the three categories and write them on the appropriate chart pages. (You may wish to establish three groups for this, one for each category.)

7. Ask participants how each of these examples of written communication has an impact on customers, and discuss how poorly written or ill-conceived written communications influence customer perception. Remind them of their responses from the written communication they received at home. Suggest to the participants that all of these written items are important for them to know about or be familiar with, as they may receive questions from customers about them.

ACTIVITY 55

Practice E-Mail Communications

Even if there is no immediate need for it, a follow-up letter or e-mail after an interaction with a customer can be a terrific way to confirm facts and details, not to mention saying thanks. Customers judge online service by how easy it is to contact a company and how quickly and accurately the company answers e-mail questions.

PURPOSE:

✓ To review recommendations for writing customer-friendly e-mail

✓ To establish standards for departmental e-mails

✓ To consider the customer's perspective

TIME: 30 minutes (This is a good exercise to pair with Activity 56.)

DIRECTIONS:

1. Make copies of Activity 55, listing recommendations for writing effective e-mail, along with the e-mail sample, and distribute to the group.

2. Discuss different aspects of this handout, such as:
   - What special effects (emoticons, colors, font sizes, capitals or block letters, text messaging abbreviations) are available to use? How might a customer interpret these?
   - What acronyms, buzzwords, and jargon do we use in our company or industry? How might these terms be confusing to an average customer?

- What is the value of reviewing an e-mail prior to clicking the "send" button?

- What are the review functions available in our software system?

- What does "friendly" mean to you? What actions cross the line of friendliness to being too informal or chatty in e-mail communications?

- Does everyone have an automatic signature? What should be included in that?

3. Bring up the subject of response time. Ask the group what it thinks the goal should be for good e-mail response time. Should that standard be the same for internal and external customers? Should it vary based on the customer request or problem, or perhaps on the customer's value to the organization (revenue contributed, longevity as customer)?

4. Examine the components of typical e-mail messages and establish some guidelines for each type. For example, should there always be a subject line? Should an e-mail be no longer than one screen? If an e-mail is longer, should it be converted into an attachment referenced in the body of the e-mail? Should the writer make the message's main point within the first two paragraphs?

5. Review the agreements you have made about e-mail standards and ask for a volunteer to list these, prepare copies of the list, and distribute the lists to the whole group.

Guidelines for Customer-Friendly E-Mail

Why do we write?

- To confirm understanding

- To create documentation

- To solidify relationships

When responding to e-mail, the standard reply time expectation for business is about eight hours, but more companies are adopting a four-hour standard. First and foremost, your goal should be to let customers know that their message has been received. Beyond that, if you can't achieve a same-day reply, let customers

This activity is available at: www.amacombooks.org/go/101ActDKYSOS
© 2009 AMACOM, a division of American Management Association.

know and provide an estimated response time. And make sure to deliver on that promise. Nothing kills customer trust faster than saying we're going to do something, then not following through.

Here are a few tips for e-mail communication:

1. Avoid use of emoticons, or symbols like the smiley face :)

2. Avoid the "special effects" available with most software programs. Stick to capitals and lowercase letters and a simple easy-to-read type font.

3. Don't YELL at customers by using all capital letters or boldface type.

4. Avoid acronyms, buzzwords, and jargon unless they are commonly known in your customer's company or industry.

5. Reread your e-mail before you click the "send" button for correct tone, spelling, grammar, and length. Avoid sending e-mail when you are in an angry or agitated state; let your heels cool before hitting that "send" button.

6. Don't get too friendly. Remember that you are in a business setting. Your goal should be to strike a tone that is efficient but not "officious." Your e-mail also should sound as if it comes from a real person, not a robot.

7. Every component of e-mail creates an impression:

   • *Subject line*—make it clear and focused for easy retrieval

   • *Greeting*—include an opening that is friendly. If you don't know the person, use Mr., Ms., Mrs., Dr.

   • *Content*—write a concise, positive message. Make sure you restate the reason for inquiry, reference to dates, and other relevant information so the reader can put the message in its proper context. It's also important to get to the point as quickly as possible.

   • *Sign-off*—sign as you would any business letter. Include your contact information for easy reference.

Dear Mr. Jones,

Let me first apologize for the problem you experienced. It must have been very disappointing for the flowers to have been delivered late to your wife for her big day. I am looking into the problem and will work to ensure it doesn't happen again.

    I realize Acme can't fully make up for the late delivery, but we hope you use the attached gift certificate to give us another chance. Acme would very much appreciate your letting us know how we did the next time you order flowers.

    Acme prides itself on delivering great service to our customers and, again, apologizes for falling short of your expectations.

    If I can be of further assistance, please feel free to contact me in the customer service group at 1-800-ACMECOM, ext. 204.

Sincerely,
Mario Juarez, CSR
Acme Flowers Internet Group
Mjuarez@acmeflowers.com

This activity is available at: www.amacombooks.org/go/101ActDKYSOS
© 2009 AMACOM, a division of American Management Association.

E-Mail Etiquette

When writing e-mail, think about the nature of the person who is on the receiving end of your message, what outcome do you want to encourage, your relationship with the individual, and how you want to present yourself. It's important that e-mail communicates a message efficiently yet does not come across as impersonal or cold.

PURPOSE:

✓ To practice rewriting e-mail messages to make them more customer-friendly

✓ To establish the right tone in e-mail communications

✓ To consider what the customer's perception will be of your e-mail

TIME: 20 minutes (Consider combining this with Activity 55 for added impact.)

DIRECTIONS:

1. Distribute copies of Activity 56.

2. Ask participants to form small groups of two or three. Have them review the examples on the handout, then rewrite them in a more customer-friendly manner, conforming to e-mail standards that you communicate. Acknowledge that they will have to make up some information to complete the e-mail. Suggest that they use your business products and services as a guide when rewriting the messages. Allow 5 to 7 minutes.

3. Ask each group to read their rewritten e-mails, concentrating on different people's version of one example at a time. Allow for two or three responses for each e-mail.

4. Ask participants how frequently e-mails are sent by them that are poorly written, incomplete, contain spelling or grammatical errors, take too long to get to the point, or are too informal. What does this say about us as an organization? What might customers' perceptions be of our organization as a result?

5. Ask participants what changes they will make to improve their e-mail communications.

Practice E-Mail Communications

The following e-mail messages require rewriting or editing to meet a professional standard of communication. Work with your partner to revise these examples.

Example 1

Subject:	Info you wanted

Hey john, got the info you needed. The transaction will go tomorrow as indicated in the system. Hope that's what you needed to know. Call me if its not.

Later,
Beth J :)

Your rewrite: _____

_____

_____

Example 2

Subject:	Cleared up the problem

Shari,
I think we cleared up the problem. If your computer is bad, be sure to contact us and we come fix it.

Raul Gomez

Your rewrite: _____

_____

_____

Example 3

Subject:	UR 2 Funny

GR8 2 TALK 2 U ♥ THE STORY (LOL) WILL GET ANSWER 2 U SOON

ANDI

Your rewrite: _____

_____

_____

Communication Sensitivity

It can be tough enough to meet the demands and soothe the frustrations of customers who share the same language, use the same jargon, or have the same business customs that you do. Differences in gender or cultural or ethnic background can add another dimension to the challenge. We need to adjust our communications and service styles based on cues that customers give to us.

PURPOSE:

✓ To understand how quickly perceptions and assumptions are formed

✓ To recognize the impact of stereotyping on communications

TIME: 20 minutes (Combine this with Activity 58 for greater impact.)

DIRECTIONS:

1. Remind participants that we all have biases, prejudices, and stereotypes, but they need to be set aside when serving customers.

2. Ask participants to look at the pictures in Activity 57. Explain that the woman is a customer; the man is a service provider.

3. Assign one person (the woman) in the picture to half of the group and the other person (the man) to the other half of the group. Ask people to make notes about their assigned person in response to the following questions:

- Given the body language and facial expressions, what might the customer (the woman) be thinking or wanting to say to the service provider?
- What might be her perceptions of him?
- What might the service provider (the man) be thinking or wanting to say to the customer?
- What might be his perceptions of her?

4. First, solicit the responses from the group assigned to the customer. Follow up by getting the responses for the service provider. Use the following questions to debrief the group:

- How do you categorize the responses—positive or negative? (Most will be negative.)
- With these perceptions, how would you describe the customer/ service provider relationship?
- What is likely to happen in this relationship in terms of ongoing business?
- How might this situation be changed?
- When have you been in a similar situation with a customer?

ACTIVITY **58**

It's a Small World

When we label people, we hinder our ability to understand what they're really saying. We base our stereotypes on many factors: age, race, ethnicity, gender, regional or foreign accents, appearance, even the vehicle a person drives. When our stereotypes take over, they inhibit our ability to listen accurately to our customers. With awareness of our own biases and prejudices, we can better work to neutralize them and serve all customers the way they wish to be served.

PURPOSE:

✓ To heighten awareness of personal biases and stereotypes

✓ To identify the impact of our treatment on customers

✓ To build a plan for personal change

TIME: 20 minutes (This activity may be combined with Activity 57 for greater impact, but use it *after* Activity 57—the sequence is important.)

DIRECTIONS:

1. Explain to participants the format of Activity 58. Discuss how this activity is designed to create awareness, not to judge anyone or to assign blame for thoughts or actions.

2. Remind participants that they will not be asked to talk about their prejudices, but to discuss the impact certain actions can have on customers. They should feel comfortable in being honest about this.

3. Distribute copies of Activity 58 and allow 7 to 10 minutes for participants to complete the form.

4. To debrief, use the following questions (remember, participants do not need to declare their stereotypes unless they choose to):

  • What did you learn about yourself?

  • How do stereotypes get in the way of providing *Knock Your Socks Off Service?*

  • What did you identify as a change in behavior going forward?

5. Congratulate participants for their candor and willingness to explore this topic. Encourage them to make any changes they identified.

Stereotypes

  • **Column A,** list several stereotypes or assumptions. (We've listed a few to get you started.)

  • **Column B,** describe your assumptions about people who fit the stereotype.

  • **Column C,** describe how you think about or treat people who fit the stereotype.

  • **Column D,** write a statement describing how you will treat that person in the future.

A. Person	B. My Assumption	C. My Past Treatment	D. My Future Treatment
People in their 70s	Old, slow, hard of hearing	Called them "dear." Talked louder to them.	Stop calling them "dear." Talk in normal tone of voice.
Teenagers			
People with foreign accents			
People who speak slowly			
People who wear "biker" clothes			
People who have multiple piercings			

The Generational Divide

Ensuring customers of various ages and eras receive service "their way" starts with understanding the distinct characteristics, attitudes, and life-shaping events that define them. As with all things in life, there'll be exceptions to every rule, so you'll want to stay flexible and adapt your approach to perceived variations in each generation.

PURPOSE:

✔ To learn the characteristics that define each generation

✔ To apply generational preferences to service style

✔ To review the current customer mix by generation

TIME: 30 minutes—10 minutes outside of work, 20 minutes in meeting

DIRECTIONS:

1. In preparation for the upcoming meeting, ask your associates to use three questions regarding service preferences (listed in Part A of Activity 59) to interview three different people from three separate generations.

2. At the meeting, review with the group the information about the targeted generations given in Part B of Activity 59.

3. Ask the participants to describe the results of their interviews. Ask the following questions as they present the information:

- How does what the interviewee said match the generational profile?

- What does this tell you about how each generation wants to receive service?
- What might you need to do differently when dealing with customers from different generations?

4. Next, ask participants to use Part C of Activity 59 to consider their current customers and list some of them by the generations they represent. Allow 3 minutes for this.

Ask the following questions:

- What clues do you have that the customer belongs to a particular generation?
- How have you treated the customer in the past?
- What might you change about how you deal with this customer in the future?

PART A

Service Considerations of the Different Generations			
	Generation 1	Generation 2	Generation 3
What is important to you in the service you receive?			
What frustrates you when it comes to customer service?			
What might a service provider do to exceed your expectations?			
What generational group does this person represent?			

PART B

The list on the next page is adapted from *The Xers & The Boomers: From Adversaries to Allies,* by Claire Raines and Jim Hunt (Crisp Publications, 2000).

Tips for Serving Veterans

1. Don't rush things. Take your time for a relaxed pace.

2. Establish rapport by being respectful in the old-fashioned way: "Please," "Thank you," "Mr.," "Mrs.," "Sir," and "Ma'am."

3. Watch your language—good grammar, clear enunciation, no profanity.

4. Be a bit more formal. Create a respectful distance between you and your customer.

5. Avoid being overly chummy or too personal.

Tips for Serving Baby Boomers

1. Be personable, especially in your greeting. Boomers may not feel like taking time to "visit," but will appreciate the warmth of an almost-chummy greeting.

2. If you know her or his name, use it in your greeting. Most Boomers like to be "known" and enjoy name recognition.

3. Take time to "check in." Find out from a Boomer how s/he is doing.

4. Treat the customer like a friend.

5. If the customer is a regular, give her or him something extra to ensure continued patronage.

Tips for Serving Generation X'ers

1. Be efficient. Competence is more important to most Gen-X'ers than schmoozing.

2. Gen-X'ers tend to ask lots of questions, so make yourself available to share information. Know your stuff so that you can give correct facts, figures, and details.

3. Don't hover. Back off and allow Gen-X'ers to make decisions for themselves.

4. Don't think you're not doing a good job just because a Gen-X'er isn't being warm and friendly to you—it may just be his or her way.

5.   Allow Gen-X'ers to be "anonymous" if you suspect they want to be anonymous.

Tips for Serving Millennials

1.   Be respectful. No one likes to be talked down to or condescended to just because s/he is young.

2.   Be sensitive to clashes between Gen-X'ers and Millennials. The generation gap can cause fireworks. Millennials typically find Gen-X'ers too edgy.

3.   Pick up the pace; look lively. Millennials like to be entertained. They find methodical people boring and long lines excruciating.

4.   Find out and talk to a Millennial about her or his interests.

PART C

The following questions can help you deliver more effective service to the different generations in your organization.

1.   What generation (or generations) are most of your customers from?

_____

_____

2.   When it comes to customer service, how do you think most of them want to be treated?

_____

_____

3.   What are the three specific things you might do to improve service for your dominant (largest) generational group?

_____

_____

4.   Is there another generation you'd like to target for improved service? How might you enhance or modify service to appeal to this group?

_____

_____

ACTIVITY **60**

Generations at Work

The ability to "get inside the heads" of customers is essential to delivering memorable service, and never more so than when serving customers from different generations. Let this activity help you think this through.

PURPOSE:

✓ To learn how different generations want to be served

✓ To practice different styles based on generational differences

✓ To develop an individual plan to change/improve behaviors suited to different generations

TIME: 30 minutes (This activity may be combined with Activity 59 as additional application.)

DIRECTIONS:

1. If you have not done Activity 59, review the information in Part B of Activity 59 with your group to discuss generational differences.

2. Ask participants to select a partner to role-play some scenarios that target generational differences and the corresponding changes in service strategy.

3. Ask the pairs to determine who will be the service provider and who will be the customer for the first round. Distribute copies of Activity 60 and ask participants to review only their role for the first situation. Allow 4 to 5 minutes for the role-play.

4. Ask participants to switch roles, then review their specific role for the second situation and do another role-play. Allow 4 to 5 minutes.

5. Ask the following questions to debrief:
   * What was different about each generation's responses and how they prefer service?
   * What was difficult for you as the service provider in responding to the needs of different generations of customers?
   * How might you change your service approach based on their different generations?

SITUATION 1
Internal Customer

* **Service Provider.** You work in the systems customer support function at your company. You pick up the phone to hear an older employee who is practically hyperventilating over the implementation of new software. This new system is pretty sweet from your perspective. It is fast, offers access to more data than ever before on two synchronized screens, and captures more data from operator input. It is state of the art and really will make the user's job easier. The caller is asking for help to better understand the system. Your immediate thought is that the caller will never get the new program. You anticipate this call taking quite a while.

   Your mission is to listen for the feeling behind the words. Ask good open-ended questions to find out how you might assist the caller. Try to soothe any concerns the customer might have.

* **Customer.** You are on the phone with your systems customer support function. A rather young voice is on the other end of the line. You are in your late 50s and are a long-term employee at the company. You have largely kept pace with new technologies introduced to the organization, but recently the pace of change has accelerated and another new software upgrade has been implemented. This new system requires dual screens and the need to enter a significant amount of information in a short period of time. The whole upgrade has caused a lot of stress and anxiety for you. You are considering the possibility of quitting because you don't think you can handle it.

   Your mission is to listen for the service provider to acknowledge your anxiety and thoughtfully walk you through the new system. The service provider should be respectful using the standard "niceties" like "please," "thank you," "you're welcome," and of course—your name. Any extras the service provider adds will be helpful and appreciated (like an offer to call any time or hard copy instructions for using elements of the system).

SITUATION 2
External Customer

- **Service Provider.** You work at a very reputable carpet store offering both sales and installation. The customer who has approached you is one you have seen in the store often. Guessing the customer to be in his early 40s, you are impressed with the selection of samples taken home for review. This buying process has gone on for several weeks. Now the customer is ready to order. The regular salesperson who has been helping the individual has the day off. You jump in to take the order, whereupon the situation begins to unravel. What the customer is asking for isn't an option with this carpet. The customer wants the higher grade carpet in a premade runner for the stairs. The premade runners come only in the standard grade carpet. As you deliver the news, the customer becomes more and more frustrated. The barrage of questions is getting to be a bit overwhelming.

  Your mission is to strive to keep your patience intact while applying the specific service suggestions for the customer's generation.

- **Customer.** As part of a remodel of your home, you decide to get new carpeting for the stairs and living room. After taking home what seems like a ton of carpet samples, you have made the final decision. As you return to the shop to place your order, you find out that what you think is available really isn't. The whole sample board is very confusing. As the salesperson keeps saying no, you are getting more and more frustrated. You have your heart set on a specific look and now it doesn't seem like that can happen. You just want someone to straighten this all out. Oh, you neglected to tell them about your three-week deadline, too. In this role you are a Generation X'er—early 40s.

  Your mission is to listen for the service provider to be direct and clear in his explanations and willing to answer all of your questions. If the service provider becomes demeaning or belittling, you get angry.

ACTIVITY **61**

Saying "No," Positively

It's a mistake to think that good service means always saying yes to customers and co-workers. Sometimes the best, and most helpful, thing you can do is to say "no." Yet saying "no" while maintaining your partnership relationship can be challenging. This activity offers three techniques for saying no in a positive way that still meets customer expectations and keeps the relationship in good standing.

PURPOSE:

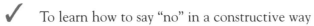 To learn how to say "no" in a constructive way

To practice using words that get the message across while maintaining the relationship

TIME: 30 minutes

DIRECTIONS:

1. Explain to participants that there are times to say "no" to the customer. Provide a few real-world examples.

2. Distribute Activity 61 to participate and review with them the three skills for saying "no" in a positive way.

3. Ask participants to form small groups so they can review and rewrite the examples provided.

4. Debrief the group by having them present their rewrites for everyone to react to.

5. Ask the group to suggest times when they need to say no in the work they do. Ask how this will help them to better serve their customers.

6. OPTIONAL: Have the participants brainstorm reasons to say no to customers. Form small groups and have each group pick a different situation and write a script for responding to customers in a positive way.

SKILL 1
Don't Assume You Can't

Service providers are willing to seek creative and innovative solutions. Before you say you can't, work with your customers to find ways that you can. Ask questions to uncover their core needs. Evaluate the inappropriate example, gather information to determine if no is the only answer, and then rewrite the appropriate response.

> CUSTOMER: I was told there was a warranty on that repair. Now you're saying that's impossible.

> SERVICE PROVIDER: I've been working here for years doing repairs. When I say a thing is impossible, it's impossible.

What the service provider should have said: _____

_____

_____

SKILL 2
Find an Alternative

Although you may not be able to do exactly what your customer is requesting, you may be able to do something else that is just as good. When you uncover the core need, you are often able to offer an alternative. Focus on gathering information so you know what alternative you can offer the customer, then rewrite your response.

> CUSTOMER: The adjustment on the system should be pretty easy. Can you walk me through it on the phone?

SERVICE PROVIDER: What do you think we are—the public library? You can get this information on our Web site. We don't have time to deal with these issues on the phone.

What the service provider should have said: _____

_____

_____

SKILL 3
Focus on the Positive

Stressing the positives reinforces the relationship. Begin and end every no with a positive thought, such as "I really appreciate your bringing this to my attention" or "I hear your concern." Focus on the positive side of the situation and rewrite the response.

CUSTOMER: This is completely unacceptable. My car has been at your place now for 4 weeks. I can't get a straight answer from anyone!

SERVICE PROVIDER: Hey, take a number. We are stacked up like cord wood for repairs.

What the service provider should have said: _____

_____

_____

SECTION THREE

Seamless *Knock Your Socks Off Service*

The behind-the-scenes actions and decisions that a customer never witnesses are some of the most important elements of delivering a *Knock Your Socks Off Service* experience. How well an incoming product order is handed off from a call center to the warehouse to the shipping department, for example, or the work that maintenance employees do to make it possible for ground crews and pilots to keep airplanes flying on time, are things that happen below the water line of the customer's vision yet are essential to their experiences of service quality.

Delivering *seamless* service, whereby employees work hand-in-glove with each other, either in the same department or in other departments, makes customer care look well orchestrated and effortless and renders the separate links in the service delivery chain invisible. This level of service begins with employees asking two questions: Where does my work go? Who is my work important to? As a *Knock Your Socks Off Service* pro, seamless service requires being a student of the company's organizational chart—knowing who the "go to" experts are to help solve vexing customer problems or answer difficult questions. There's nothing worse for customers, for example, than to call an 800 number with a problem, be placed on hold, then be transferred to someone who has no clue how to resolve the problems.

Seamless service—the kind that leads to hiccup-free experiences for customers—also requires teamwork in an atmosphere where customers' needs are placed above turf battles or personal agendas. The term *internal customer* is often used to describe relationships with co-workers in other departments, but we think the term *partner* is just as appropriate. Partnerships are about equality and teamwork, about not caring who gets the credit as long as customers are well served—concepts at the very heart of seamless service.

Finally, seamless service is about avoiding the "it's not my job" syndrome—where service professionals routinely step in to help if they see a customer in need or a co-worker struggling with a difficult task, and where they go above and beyond to ensure customers walk away from interactions feeling valued and respected.

The training activities in this section will help raise your staff's awareness of the importance of teamwork and cross-departmental cooperation—in delighting customers and building skills to ensure that customers rarely, if ever, see the seams in your service delivery process.

ACTIVITY **62**

Communicating Across Functions

How well your organization's departments work together is key to making service "magic" happen. One of the biggest challenges in cross-functional work is communicating effectively. Consider the following points to improve communication between organizational partners:

- *Priorities:* What is important to me/my work group at any given point in time

- *Roles and Responsibilities:* What I believe to be my job and the tasks I perform

- *Listening:* How well I hear, understand, and incorporate the messages that come at me

PURPOSE:

✓ To identify priorities in the work of the department
✓ To assess how department priorities fit with those of internal partners

TIME: 30 minutes

DIRECTIONS:

1. Explain to participants the need for consistent and coordinated internal service.

2. Distribute copies of Activity 62. Ask participants to take time in answering the questions. Allow 10 minutes.

3. Have participants present their responses, one question at a time. Remember, there are no right or wrong answers. These responses reflect the perceptions of the associates.

4. Together, have participants rank the priorities identified in the discussion. It is likely many priorities can be combined to form larger, more complete priorities.

5. Review with the group the roles and responsibilities in the department and clarify where there are differences in associates' perceptions of their roles.

6. Discuss how well the group listens to requests and questions from internal partners. Use the following questions to help spur discussion:

   • What type of requests, questions, or suggestions do we get from our internal partners?

   • What percentage of your work time is given to these requests?

   • How have we, as a department, incorporated the suggestions from other departments into our work processes?

   • What more might we do to react to suggestions from our internal partners for the good of external customers?

7. Ask for suggestions for what would be the next step in building a more cohesive, coordinated service strategy. Build a plan as a team.

1. What is my job function?

   _____

   _____

   _____

2. What is my role and responsibility in the department?

   _____

   _____

   _____

This activity is available at: www.amacombooks.org/go/101ActDKYSOS
© 2009 AMACOM, a division of American Management Association.

3. How does our department fit into the overall structure of the company?

    _____

    _____

    _____

4. What are my long- and short-term priorities?

    _____

    _____

    _____

5. How do these priorities fit with those of my internal partners?

    _____

    _____

    _____

6. How well do I (or my department) listen to the requests, questions, and suggestions of our partners?

    _____

    _____

    _____

7. What might I be able to do differently to improve the communications and coordination between our department and our partners?

    _____

    _____

    _____

ACTIVITY **63**

Hitting the Target

Seamless Service is about understanding how your job fits into the bigger picture that is the customer's experience. With all the stress and pressure to meet deadlines and customer expectations, it is easy to stop listening while pushing your priorities as the most important, because they are the job you do. However, doing this may fail to take into account what is best for the customer, whether it be an internal or external customer.

PURPOSE:

✓   To define what we control and what we don't

✓   To discuss and agree on priorities in the work of the department

TIME: 20 minutes (A great activity to pair with Activity 62.)

DIRECTIONS:

1. Remind participants of the goal of providing seamless service. Everyone in the organization should have the best interests of the customer in mind.

2. Ask participants how often they are frustrated because of a misstep or breakdown in another department. Allow a minute or two of whining.

3. Distribute copies of Part A of Activity 63 and ask participants to label the circles as you suggest. The inside circle is "What I control." The next circle is "What I influence." And the outer circle is labeled "Everything else."

4. Ask participants to think about the job they do and to list those tasks in the center and middle circles, as appropriate.

5. Now, explain that if something they are frustrated about is not in one of those two circles, it falls into the outer circle labeled "Everything else." Stress that it is important they let go of those frustrations. It is likely they can neither control nor influence them.

6. To help focus on the impact on customers of what participants do in their jobs, ask them to answer the questions in Part B of Activity 63. Allow 5 minutes.

7. Open up a discussion by asking the following questions:
- What types of things did you list that you control?
- What are the things you listed that you influence?
- What did you identify as your role and responsibility?
- What ideas did you identify to open communications and strive for Seamless Service?

8. Ask participants to identify one action they will take to move toward Seamless Service.

PART A

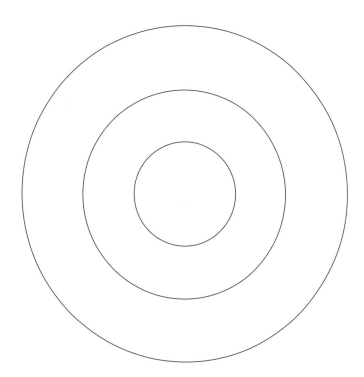

PART B

1. What do I control?

    _____

    _____

    _____

    _____

2. What do I influence?

    _____

    _____

    _____

    _____

3. What is my role and my responsibility?

    _____

    _____

    _____

    _____

4. What am I able to do to improve communications between groups
    for the express purpose of creating seamless customer service?

    _____

    _____

    _____

    _____

ACTIVITY **64**

Visit an Internal Customer

Customers exist both inside and outside the organization. There is much to learn about the workings of the other functions and departments in your company. How do they interact with external customers? What happens to the work that you pass on to them? What might your department be doing that causes frustration or aggravation for your closest internal partners?

PURPOSE:

✓ To learn about other functions in your organization and how they work together

✓ To broaden the business perspective of associates

✓ To better understand the needs of another function in the organization

TIME: 30 minutes

DIRECTIONS:

1. As a group, discuss and list which departments or personnel you consider to be your key internal partners. Remind participants that customers exist both outside and inside your company.

2. Ask participants what they know about the functions of the other departments you have listed.

3. Remind participants that the idea of this exercise is to always be learning. Have them select one department to visit and learn about their operations. Encourage them to use the questions in Activity 64 to trigger learning.

4. Once they have completed their visits, ask participants to prepare a short presentation on what they have learned. This presentation may be done in any format.

Visit An Internal Customer

1. What department did you visit?

   _____

   _____

2. What is the primary function of that department?

   _____

   _____

3. How does your department interact with this group?

   _____

   _____

4. How does the external customer interact with this department?

   _____

   _____

5. What unintentional frustrations might your department cause for this group?

   _____

   _____

6. What two things that you learned might improve how your group serves this department?

   _____

   _____

7. What surprised you about this department?

   _____

   _____

ACTIVITY **65**

It's Not My Job

Providing Seamless Service is about taking the initiative to help customers even when that duty appears to fall outside the boundaries of your normal job. Nothing says *Knock Your Socks Off Service* to customers or co-workers like a willingness to go out of your way to do the little extras to help meet their needs.

PURPOSE:

✓ To experience the "not my job" frustration that customers or co-workers feel

✓ To practice taking ownership when a customer or co-worker is in need

TIME: 30 minutes

DIRECTIONS:

1. Ask participants what happens when an employee says or indicates "It's not my job" to either internal partners or external customers. Look for responses like, "It makes people mad or frustrated," "It makes the customer think you don't know what you're talking about," "It makes more work for other people," "It causes that person to lose the respect of co-workers," "The company could lose a customer."

2. Explain to participants that this activity is designed to have them experience the difference between taking ownership and not. Ask them to choose a partner for a role-play exchange.

3. Have partners decide who will go first. Distribute copies of the activity below to each pair. Ask them to read their role in the first situation, then allow 3 to 4 minutes for the role-play.

4. Without any discussion, have partners reverse roles and role-play the second situation, again allowing 3 to 4 minutes for the interaction.

5. Discuss with the whole group the difference in these role-plays. Use the following questions to help the discussion:

   • What was the difference in the feel of these two situations?

   • How did the customer react to the difference in the way the service provider handled the situation?

   • What did you learn about taking responsibility for helping the customer?

   • How do these situations mirror what happens in our organization?

   • What if these customers are internal partners? Does that make a difference?

   • (If you are in a call center, this may apply.) How do you handle the pressure of meeting the customer's needs and keeping your focus on the call length established by the company?

   • How do you handle the pressure of going above and beyond— and still getting your work done?

SITUATION 1

The point of this role-play is to avoid taking ownership of the customer's complaint. In other words, you want someone else to deal with it.

• **Service Provider.** You are a call center rep on a high-volume call line. The call you just picked up didn't start well. The caller is not sure who he needs to talk to about a billing problem—it might not be a billing problem at all. It may be an inaccurate order or a picking problem in the warehouse. You explain to the customer that the best thing to do is to start with the billing department because you don't have access to that information. You start to give the customer the name and phone number of the person to whom you are transferring the call when the caller interrupts and stops you. Continuing on to provide more information, you now decide that the best place to send the customer is to the order entry department because there seems to be more confusion on the order than a billing error. Now, you start to give the customer the name and number of someone in order entry and are ready to transfer the call. Again, the customer interrupts with increased frustration and explains that the order copy was actually correct—so might the problem have happened in the warehouse when pulling the order? Given this new information, you suggest a transfer to the warehouse manager to research the pulling slips they keep on file. Again, the customer is frustrated that this can't be solved with just one call. Why are you called the "customer service department" if you can't help?

- **Customer.** You are a customer with a vexing problem. You aren't sure where to start in the company, so you contact customer service. After being placed on hold for about 12 minutes, and hearing the message that "you're a valuable customer so please stay on the line" so many times you're ready to shatter the phone, you finally get through to a human being. You recently placed an order with this supplier and the order arrived all wrong. The invoice enclosed with the shipment doesn't match the product you received. You changed the order on the phone with the rep because there are back orders on some products, so it might be an order-entry problem. But, when you quickly reviewed the online order, it appeared to be correct. This might indicate a picking problem in the warehouse. You really don't want to be transferred, so when the rep suggests a transfer, you interrupt and get increasingly more frustrated. You keep asking the rep why she can't help; you wonder why they call her department "customer service." Try to "guilt" the service provider to take charge of this problem and get it figured out and get back to you.

SITUATION 2

The point of this role-play is to take responsibility for the customer's needs and create a positive outcome.

- **Service Provider.** You work at the service desk of your local big box retailer. A customer approaches the desk with several products in hand. She is direct and thorough in her explanation. Her daughter was just married locally and received these items as gifts. Because her daughter didn't have time to return the gifts before leaving for her new home in another state, you are here to return the items in exchange for a gift card. Because the items were purchased online, there are packing slips in the boxes, but no receipts. You explain to the customer that she will need to go to the kiosk and print receipts. Once the receipts are printed she may or may not be able to return the items at the store. After all, not every product bought from the Web site can be returned at the brick-and-mortar store.

After assisting the customer with printing the receipts, you begin to process the returns. The customer asks you questions you can't answer, so you suggest the 800 line as her best chance to get answers. However, you encounter all kinds of problems with the receipts. Meanwhile, the customer is getting more and more frustrated because of the length of time it is taking. She indicates that she is now late for an appointment. She says it is ridiculous for a store of this magnitude to have such different return practices for items bought in-store and online. Not giving up, you contact the Web site help line to eventually process the returns. While the customer is ultimately satisfied and ends up praising you, the situation took an extraordinary amount of time—45 minutes.

- **Customer.** Your daughter was married a week ago, and several gifts arrived at your home after she had left to live in her new home in another state. In phone conversations, the two of you decided that it's easiest to return the items to the big box retailer for a store gift card. She will then purchase these items in her new community and save the shipping costs. As you approach the service desk, you are confident that you have everything in order, only to be told that there are no receipts and they must be printed at the kiosk. And, once you print the receipts, the store may or may not be able accept the returns. That in itself makes you furious. Asking for help with printing the receipts, you eventually complete that task—after grumbling a bunch that you have to do all the work. You repeatedly ask the service provider why there are no gift receipts in these boxes. The service provider can't answer the question, and continues to defer your questions to the 800 line for the best chance at getting answers. Compared to regular store returns, this seems to be taking an unusual amount of time. The service provider is getting support from the Web site help line, but you get more and more frustrated. If the service provider assures you everything will be fine, apologizes for the length of time it is taking, or makes small talk with you, you may back off. After all, the service provider is doing what he can to handle the situation. Once this exchange is completed, you are satisfied and ask the service provider for his name to commend him on the 800 line for all the patience and perseverance demonstrated.

ACTIVITY **66**

Mindbenders

One of the most exciting elements of working with a team is learning that it's not all about you! Each team member brings something unique to the table, offering something that you cannot. Being able to identify the strengths of other team members is a great asset to you individually and to the organization as a whole.

PURPOSE:

✓ To recognize your strengths as well as the strengths of your co-workers

✓ To open your mind to other kinds of thinking

✓ To learn the value of planning before doing

TIME: 20 minutes

DIRECTIONS

1. Explain to participants that this activity is about having fun while working together.

2. Ask the participants to form small groups. Distribute copies of Part A of Activity 66 and ask them to work together to complete the questions and solve the problems. (Answers are given in Part B.) Allow 10 minutes.

3. Reassemble the group. Use the following questions to have a discussion:
   - How did your team decide to approach the activity?
   - Whose skills surprised you?

- Were there people on your team who were stronger in some activities than in others? Where among the group were the skill strengths?
- How did all the team members engage in the activity?
- How is this like working together on a daily basis?
- How did you resolve conflicts or reach consensus on answers?
- What did you learn about yourself and the others in your group?

4. If you have prizes to give out, they can be a fun way to end the activity.

PART A

Assign the appropriate type of visual to the information written in each of the three scenarios that follow.

1. Greet the customer, ask for his account number, pull up the account on your computer, then ask the customer how you might be of service.

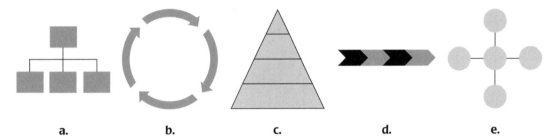

    a.   **b.**   **c.**   **d.**   **e.**

2. Only 7 percent of a person's message is communicated through text. The rest of the message is communicated through subtext (38%) and context (55%).

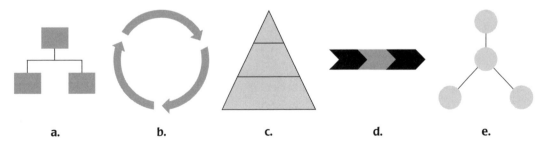

    a.   **b.**   **c.**   **d.**   **e.**

3. You take the next call in the queue, manage the customer's issue, notate the resolution in the client's account notes, offer a cross sell, then close the call.

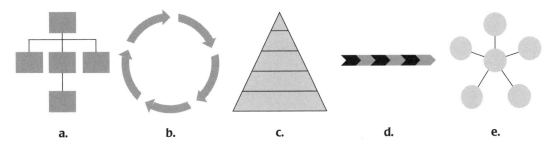

    a.   **b.**   **c.**   **d.**   **e.**

4. A manager is approached by one of his most productive employees. The employee's father has recently moved in with him and requires supervision. The employee explains that unless he is allowed to work from home two days a week, he will have to seek employment with a competitor whom he knows allows employees to work from home. After assessing the replacement cost of the employee, the manager decides to allow the employee to work from home two days a week. Which adage best describes the manager's decision?

   a. Anything worth having is worth fighting for

   b. You get what you pay for

   c. A bird in the hand is worth two in the bush

   d. In order to run with the big dogs you have to get off the porch

5. One day at the water cooler, Gordon tells his co-workers about a training class he is taking and how useful he finds the information for his work. Over the next two days, Gordon's manager receives several requests from his direct reports to be sent to the same training. The manager decides to fulfill each request separately rather than arrange for the trainer to come in-house and deliver the class to all employees at two-thirds the cost. Which adage best describes the manager's decision?

   a. A penny saved is a penny earned

   b. Penny wise, pound foolish

c. You can lead a horse to water but you can't make him drink

d. Timing is everything

6. Solve the following equations:

a. 100 Y = F B Field

b. 4 L C = G L

c. S + H + Sm + T + T = 5 Ss

d. S + S + F + W = S of the Y

e. S + A + J + N = M with 30 D

PART B

Answers to Part A (You may want to give *one* answer for problem 6 so participants realize how they work.)

1. d

2. c

3. b

4. c

5. b

6. a. 100 Yards = Football Field

b. 4-Leaf Clover = Good Luck

c. See + Hear + Smell + Taste + Touch = 5 Senses

d. Spring + Summer + Fall + Winter = Seasons of the Year

e. September + April + June + November = Months with 30 Days

ACTIVITY **67**

It's All About Kindness

The movie *Pay It Forward* illustrates what the power of a good deed multiplied can accomplish. The same holds true for performing *Knock Your Socks Off Service*. Management guru Tom Peters suggested that making a commitment to perform one 10-minute outstanding service act each day—and encouraging your colleagues to do the same—can help turn your organization into a service powerhouse. Think of it: in a company with 100 employees, a simple 10-minute courteous act each day (to co-workers or external customers) translates into some 24,000 kind acts each year. Talk about making an impact!

PURPOSE:

✓ To discover how easy it is to perform a courteous act

✓ To consider the impact such acts have on others

✓ To create systems and reminders that help you keep performing these acts of exceptional service

TIME: 70 minutes individual time, 20-minute group meeting

DIRECTIONS:

1. Explain to participants that, in our busy work lives, we often forget about doing kind things for others. This activity will reinforce how important doing that is.

2. Distribute copies of Activity 67 and ask participants, during the next seven work days, to keep a log of their exceptional acts of customer service.

3. At the end of the seven days, reassemble the team and see what changes have occurred, both inside and outside your department. Consider the following questions:

- What feels different in the department?
- How do you feel about your job after these seven days versus the week prior?
- What made the acts of exceptional service difficult for you to perform?
- How easy will it be to keep up this behavior?
- How did or will you react when others don't repay your acts of exceptional service?
- What will you do if you don't get a thank you?

4. Ask participants how they plan to incorporate this concept in their everyday work.

This activity is available at: www.amacombooks.org/go/101ActDKYSOS
© 2009 AMACOM, a division of American Management Association.

Exceptional Service Log

Day	Act of Exceptional Customer Service	Customer's or Co-Worker's Reaction	How I Felt	How I Will Handle Similar Situations in the Future
Day 1				
Day 2				
Day 3				
Day 4				
Day 5				
Day 6				
Day 7				

ACTIVITY **68**

Details, Details, Details

The little details make all the difference, no matter what kind of job we do. It's how we look and how our workplace looks. It's how we speak and what we say. It's all the little extra courtesies and comforts we build into the service experience that can separate us from our competitors in customers' eyes.

PURPOSE:

✓   To observe other organizations' attention to details

✓   To apply these observations in your organization

TIME: Two meetings—one 10 minutes, one 20 minutes; observation time varies

DIRECTIONS:

1. Spend a few minutes discussing those businesses that associates believe focus on the details. Some examples everyone might recognize include Disney theme parks, Wegmans market, and Ritz-Carlton Hotels. Ask about businesses in your specific industry as well, and those who operate locally that are recognized for their attention to detail.

2. Explain to participants that they will learn what other businesses do to focus on details by becoming secret shoppers. Explain that this is the activity for the next several days: to observe how other service providers pay attention to the details.

3. Ask participants how they envision the role of a secret shopper. Listen for responses like, "Make notes about what other organizations do to focus on details," "Review signage, printed materials, and work areas," "Listen to the words their employees use," "Look for the little extras

that might not be elsewhere," "Ask an employee what is most important in the work they do."

4. Ask participants to pick two organizations from your list of businesses. They will contact both of them in the next week, one by phone and the other in person. They will be in the role of secret shoppers; ask them to keep detailed notes of what they observe, using the form that follows. Remind them that their focus is on attention to detail and how these providers demonstrate sensitivity to what customers might feel is important.

5. At the follow-up meeting, ask participants to share both negative and positive observations. Keep a list of both on separate chart papers.

6. Review the list of negative points and remind everyone these are behaviors and situations you want to avoid!

7. Review the list of positives and ask the group how this attention to detail might be incorporated into the work they do. Ask each person to commit to one change in behavior and to add one important improvement to a detail in their everyday work.

List the types of behaviors you observe that focus on details. Then rate the importance of that behavior to you (1 = low importance, 5 = high importance).

Face-to-Face Contact	
Positive Attention to Detail	**Negative Attention to Detail**
Example: At the restaurant, the manager asked how our food and service were.	Example: Our server called a mixed group of people "guys." The women were offended.

Phone Contact	
Positive Attention to Detail	**Negative Attention to Detail**
Example: The person who answered my call asked a couple of good questions before transferring me to someone else.	Example: The service provider never used my name.

ACTIVITY **69**

Creating a Cycle of Service

It's critical when delivering *Knock Your Socks Off Service* to know what the customer perceives as *Knock Your Socks Off Service*. If you're not on the same page, then you could easily be making incorrect assumptions. Companies, and service professionals, assume a lot if they don't take a walk in the customer's shoes. By mapping out a *Cycle of Service,* you can identify all of the "Moments of Truth" that a customer experiences—times that determine his willingness to keep doing business with you.

PURPOSE:

✓ To see work processes from the customer's point of view

✓ To build consistency in work processes

TIME: 10 minutes

DIRECTIONS:

1. Explain to participants the concepts of a Cycle of Service and Moments of Truth (see Part A of Activity 69 for definitions). Point out that these experiences are best considered from the customer's perspective, not from the inside looking out. After all, it is the customer who ultimately determines whether we get to keep our jobs.

2. Review with the group the example in Part B of Activity 69, based on an experience as a customer. For example, checking into a hotel is an act that everyone can relate to. Recognize that there may be more subtle steps in between, but that the point of the cycle of service is to capture the customer experiences to meet a particular need.

3. Distribute copies of Part C of Activity 69, containing a blank Cycle of Service. Ask participants to think of one work process they use repeatedly—it should not be the most complex or the easiest, but something in between. Have them individually write out the steps in this service process. The trigger at the top of the page may help with this. (Note: There may be more or less specific points in the particular process participants choose.)

4. In addition to asking a couple of participants to walk the group through their Cycle of Service, use the following questions to discuss the topic:

    - How hard or easy was it for you to write the service steps from the perspective of the customer?

    - Where in this cycle do most problems tend to occur for customers?

    - Where in the cycle do most problems occur for you and your service team?

5. Collect and keep the participants' Cycles of Service for future use.

PART A

Some definitions for completing this activity.

- **Cycle of Service.** A Cycle of Service starts with a specific need and ends when that need is fulfilled. It involves the customer at each moment and is the customer's Moment of Truth. An *extraordinary* Cycle of Service is one in which the customer experiences each individual Moment of Truth as positive.

- **Moment of Truth.** Any encounter a customer has with an organization during which s/he has an opportunity to form an impression or make an evaluation. The phrase comes from bull fighting—the moment of reckoning when the matador faces the bull. The key element is what the customer experiences (that is, her or his view), not what the organization thinks or is doing.

PART B

Example: Checking into a hotel

I, the customer . . .

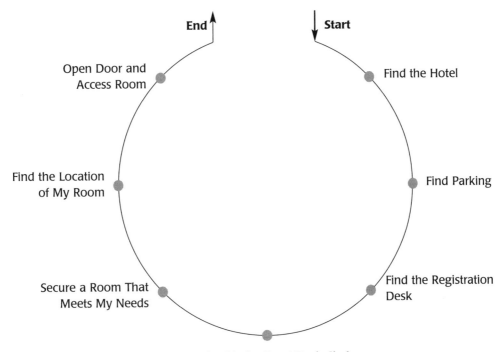

PART C

Your customer experience: _____

The customer will…

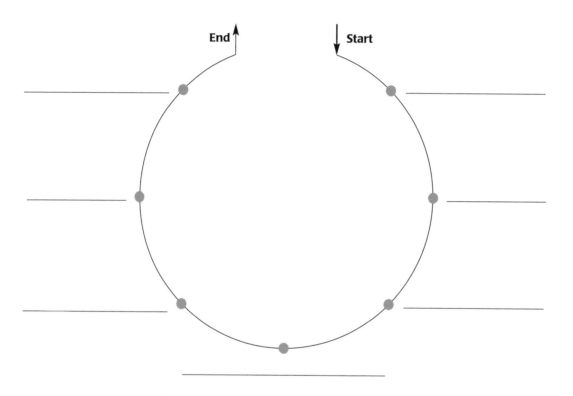

ACTIVITY **70**

Analyzing Moments of Truth

In every work process, there are certain steps that cause the most aggravation and frustration for customers. As service providers, we may not even recognize these problem areas. What can we do to raise our awareness and help eliminate those speed bumps?

PURPOSE:

✓ To identify problem spots or breakdowns that customers experience in a cycle of service

✓ To critically view a process for improvement

✓ To examine operations from the customers' eyes

TIME: 20 minutes (Activity 69 is a prerequisite for this activity.)

DIRECTIONS:

1. Explain to participants that they will work independently to perform a key Moment of Truth impact analysis on their Cycle of Service. Distribute copies of Activity 70 and use the definitions provided in Activity 69 to help participants understand what is meant by a key Moment of Truth. (A key Moment of Truth is the one step in the process that affects the most customers or causes the most frustration or aggravation for the customer.)

2. Describe to the participants what a Moment of Truth Impact Analysis is: a process of putting a microscope on a key Moment of Truth, with the goal of understanding it from the customer's perspective. Explain

that this is the first step in redesigning a service process. There are three parts to the analysis: what the customer expects to happen (that is, what would satisfy the typical customer); what would enhance a particular Moment of Truth; and what typically detracts from the experience at that Moment of Truth. Looking at their Cycle of Service, have participants select the key Moment of Truth for their analysis.

3. Participants should begin their analysis with recognition of basic customer expectations. Those expectations should be listed in column B. Explain to participants that they should start their analysis in the center column, and then work in either direction—detractors and then enhancers, or enhancers and then detractors.

4. Working with the group, identify possible enhancers. For example, what can they do to surprise the customer? Be sure that you're not simply fixing the core offering but, rather, enhancing or adding value to the customer's experience. Describe the enhancers in column C. These do not need to parallel the expectations; they may be new ideas that present themselves.

5. In column A, identify any detractors—an event or condition that causes customer frustrations or disappointments. What gets in the way of meeting the customer's expectations?

6. Select a few participants to "walk through" their analyses. Encourage the others to ask questions. Help the participants flesh out these ideas a bit. Use the following questions to help:

- How might your suggested enhancers be funded, if funding is needed? To whom would you have to speak?

- What did you learn about the customer's perspective?

- How might we incorporate these suggestions in our everyday work?

Moment of Truth Impact Analysis

A. Detractors	B. Customer Expectations	C. Enhancers

ACTIVITY **71**

Details That Make a Difference

Attention to detail is one way to manage your customers' perceptions. Focus on the details that are most important to your customers. Do you know what they are?

PURPOSE:

✓ To learn by doing

✓ To gather customer input

✓ To implement suggestions from customer feedback

TIME: 10-minute meeting, research, 30-minute meeting

DIRECTIONS:

1. When the group assembles, explain the purpose of this exercise. The challenge is to find out what details are important to customers in the work processes you do.

2. Prior to talking to customers, have participants work through the questions in Part A of Activity 71, concerning the details in the work they do.

3. Following a brief discussion, ask participants, in the next week, to talk to two or three customers. They should focus on getting feedback on what details are important to customers, related to the Moments of Truth they experience. If you have done Activity 70, use the list of Moments of Truth that the participants identified. Be sure participants

select specific moments to focus on in their research with customers. They should record their findings on the form in Part B of Activity 71.

4. When the group reassembles, ask several participants to report on their findings. Record the results on chart paper or white board.

5. At the completion of the presentations, ask the group to determine which additions or changes to the details on the list might be incorporated into the work they do.

6. Assign one suggestion each to a small group of participants. Have them brainstorm how this addition or change can be implemented. Allow 5 minutes.

7. Have each group present its suggestions. Open up the discussion to all and reach consensus on how to proceed and exactly what to change.

PART A
Participant Questions

1. When you think about attention to detail, what details are important to you?

_____

_____

_____

_____

2. When you visit other businesses, what types of little details or little extras do you notice?

_____

_____

_____

_____

3. In the work you do, what details do you provide to your customers on a regular basis?

    _____

    _____

    _____

    _____

4. What details do customers routinely ask for that you could provide on a regular basis?

    _____

    _____

    _____

    _____

PART B
Customer Interviews

Customer 1 Responses

1. When working with our organization, what details are important to you?

    _____

    _____

    _____

2. What is missing that we might add, or change what currently exists?

    _____

    _____

    _____

    _____

3.   What does our organization do well when focusing on the details of working with customers?

_____

_____

_____

_____

Customer 2 Responses

1.   When working with our organization, what details are important to you?

_____

_____

_____

_____

2.   What is missing that we might add, or change what currently exists?

_____

_____

_____

_____

3.   What does our organization do well when focusing on the details of working with customers?

_____

_____

_____

_____

ACTIVITY **72**

Value-Added Service

In today's world, sales, marketing, service, and operations share a common goal: creating and retaining customers. To create and retain customers, we have to combine good selling with good service.

PURPOSE:

✓ To connect products and services to each other

✓ To counter the myth that service and sales functions work at cross-purposes

✓ To build vocabulary and practice in this process

TIME: 20 minutes (For additional practice, pair this with Activity 73.)

DIRECTIONS:

1. Prior to the meeting, prepare a list of products or services your company offers. Put these on index cards or small pieces of paper. These items should be familiar to participants.

2. Ask participants how many of them define their job as sales. Ask them to explain why or why not.

3. Explain to participants that it is their responsibility to inform, educate, and help customers learn about new products/services, about enhancements to existing products/services, and about relationships between products and services. Review Part A of Activity 72, "Five Situations in Which Selling Is Good Service and Three Situations in Which Selling Is Not Good Service."

4. Ask participants to form small groups. Next, have a volunteer from each group draw a card from those you prepared. Explain that the card they selected is their assignment for the next part of this activity.

5. Distribute copies of Part B of Activity 72 and have the groups discuss their products/services and identify other products/services that relate to, support, or replace the product/service on the card. In the time they have, they should also prepare a script to introduce the new product, connect the two products, or explain the value of the replacement. Allow 10 minutes.

6. Ask each group to make its presentation to the others. Encourage the discussion of ideas and give recognition to each group.

7. Ask for a volunteer to collect the ideas so they can be compiled, reproduced, and distributed to the group. Ask that each participant use these ideas for the next couple of weeks to see how well they work.

PART A

Five Situations in Which Selling Is Good Service

1. When the product or service the customer is using is wrong—but you know which model, system, or approach will better fit the customer's needs and you are in a position to get it for the customer.

2. When the product or service the customer acquired from your company is right—but some other part, piece, program, or process is needed before your product or service will perform properly—"Your computer operating system is Windows 95. Our software is designed for the Vista operating system. I do know of an upgrade for Windows 95 that might work."

3. When the product or service in question is out of date—"I can send you a new widget and walk you through the repair when you receive it. I also think it would be a good idea to consider a newer model that will do the job better. The Laser XJ7 has improved circuitry and can… ."

4. When an add-on feature will forestall other problems—"I see you decided against extended warranty protection. Since you've had two problems during the warranty period, I wonder if you shouldn't reconsider that decision?"

5. When changing the customer to a different product or service will be seen as value-added or TLC—"This checking account requires a very high minimum balance. That's what caused the service charge you are concerned about. I'd like to recommend a different plan that I think will fit your needs better and save you from incurring future charges."

Three Situations in Which Selling Is Not Good Service

1. When there are no alternatives. The customer's needs cannot be met by any product or service you offer, regardless of how well you can fix the problem, answer the question, or explain the current product or service.

2. When there is no slack. You know how to solve the problem, but the customer came to you mad, has stayed mad, and obviously wants to stay mad. There is very little chance to make the customer happy, let alone sell an upgrade or a switch to a different model.

3. When there is no point. An upgrade or add-on would be totally illogical, unrelated, or inappropriate to the situation, as in, "Would you like some garlic bread to go with your cappuccino this morning?"

PART B

1. Your product/service assignment:_____

2. Identify other products/services that relate to, support, or replace this one.

    _____

    _____

3. Create a script to introduce the new product, connect the two products, or explain the value of replacement.

    _____

    _____

Good Selling Is Good Service

Selling plays an important role in many service jobs. Whether it's being asked to cross-sell company products at the end of a customer call, or to recommend relevant products or services you think may complement a customer's initial purchase, sales and service are two sides of the same coin. But how we handle that often-delicate selling task makes the difference between closing a sale and irritating customers with poorly timed or heavy-handed approaches.

PURPOSE:

✓ To review the most effective times to use selling strategies in the service process—and times to avoid selling

✓ To practice good cross-selling and up-selling techniques

✓ To stress that sales isn't about manipulation; done well, it's a higher form of customer service

TIME: 30 minutes (This activity works well with Activity 72.)

DIRECTIONS:

1. Refer participants to Activity 72, detailing the best and worst times to use selling techniques in service roles. Have participants review and provide feedback on whether they agree with those points.

2. Explain what is meant by cross-selling and up-selling. (See Part A of Activity 73.)

3. Remind participants that effective cross-selling and up-selling require knowing both company products and customer needs exceptionally well. Good cross-selling means asking good questions and listening for cues, and knowing how to match complementary products or services to initial purchases. It's also important that service professionals aren't heavy-handed in their sales approaches. The goal should be to suggest, not push, and to respect the wishes of customers who say they're not interested.

4. Stress the importance of using a different yardstick to measure sales success. In other words, it might take nine no's to get to a yes when cross-selling. It's important for your team to develop the strength to not take rejection personally and to remember that they're providing a valuable service to customers. Many customers, for example, may not be aware of options available to them that could help cut costs, increase sales, make their jobs easier, or more.

5. With that backdrop, spend 10 minutes exploring these questions with the group:

- In what situations do you find it most difficult to sell to customers? Why?

- How does it make you feel when customers don't accept your sales offers?

- In what situations have customers proved most receptive to your sales suggestions?

- What are the core products or services that we sell and service? For each, what might be an effective cross-sell? What about an up-sell?

- What are some ways we might overcome customer objections to our approaches?

6. Have participants break into pairs for a short role-play exercise (Part B of Activity 73). The pairs will trade roles of service provider and customer in each of two situations. Allow 3 to 4 minutes for each role-play.

PART A

Whether it's being asked to cross-sell company products at the end of a customer call, or to recommend relevant products or services you think may complement a customer's initial purchase, sales and service are two sides of the same coin. Following are definitions that will help you better understand both —cross-selling and up-selling.

- **Cross-selling.** When customers are sold a product or service, then are referred to related offerings that might complement their first purchase. This happens, for example, when someone buys computer software and is offered an accompanying training package, or when the coffee shop asks if you'd like a muffin to go with your cappuccino.

- **Up-selling.** When customers are considering buying something and you suggest they spend more for additional features or a different model that may better fit their needs. This happens, for example, when you are offered better tires than what you considered for only slightly more than the original cost.

PART B

Situation 1

- **Service Provider.** You're a customer service representative for a telecom company. A customer calls with a routine question about when his upcoming monthly payment for Internet service is due. During the conversation he mentions the slower-than-expected download speeds he's been experiencing for the videos and games he regularly accesses online. As he talks, you remember your company has recently introduced a "powerboost" version of its DSL service, which offers much faster downloads than the baseline DSL service the customer has. While the upgrade costs a bit more per month, it would be a good fit for the customer's needs.

  Your mission is to up-sell the customer on this new DSL service.

- **Customer.** You've made a routine call to your telecom provider because you haven't received a bill lately and are wondering when your next payment is due. When the service rep asks how your service has been working, you mention that you're surprised how slow the downloads have been for video and games, as well as uploads of digital photos. When the rep suggests upgrading to a faster but more expensive DSL service, you are curious but also skeptical: will the upgrade really be that much faster?

  Your goal is to provide some resistance or objections to the service rep's up-selling approach and seek proof that the new service will really be worth the extra cost before subscribing.

Situation 2

- **Service Provider.** A customer walks into your electronics store complaining about the new big-screen, plasma HDTV he's just bought. In the year that he's owned it he's already had problems with color functions and with a blown interior light bulb. The one-year warranty did cover repairs, but it recently expired. You ask the customer whether, given the problems, he would like to reconsider his earlier decision not to purchase the extended five-year warranty. Would he like to buy it now to cover himself into the future?

  Your mission is to convince the customer that this might be a wise purchase.

- **Customer.** You've spent the equivalent of two mortgage payments on a new big-screen HDTV, but after a year of use you've experienced some frustrating problems with it—color functions (the color wheel was defective) and a blown interior light bulb. Initially you thought buying an extended warranty was a waste of money, but you've recently realized the model you bought, because it's so new, doesn't have a repair record listed anywhere, and you know repair costs for these TVs can be very high.

  Your mission should be to question the salesperson who tries to sell you the extended warranty. You wonder whether all the big problems that could happen to the TV have already happened. And you think the extended warranty is priced a little high at 20 percent of your original sales price; you think it should be closer to 10 or 15 percent, which some competitors charge.

ACTIVITY **74**

So Many People to Thank

Saying "thank you" is as important in your service work as it was when your parents tried so hard to drum it into your head as a youngster. In your job, you need to say thanks to your customers every day. You need to sincerely value the gift of business they bring you—even if it may not be as exciting as celebrating your birthday.

PURPOSE:

✓ To remind people how easy it can be to say "thank you"

✓ To stress how saying "thank you" can boost morale of co-workers and customers

✓ To reinforce that saying thanks can make the givers feel just as good as the recipients

TIME: 30 minutes

DIRECTIONS:

1. Distribute copies of Parts A and B of Activity 74. Discuss the Part A handout. Ask participants to complete the Part B form.

2. Discuss with participants what they learned from this activity. Use the following questions to examine their responses:

   • How easy was it to identify five people to thank?

   • Who made up your list of people (external customers, co-workers, boss, internal customers)?

- Give an example of a way you plan to say "thank you" to one individual.

- How long do you anticipate this will take (target dates)?

PART A

Nine Times When You Should Thank Customers

1. *When they do business with you—every time.* It bears repeating. Customers have options every time they need a service or product. It's easy to take regular and walk-in customers for granted. Don't. Thank them for choosing to do business with you.

2. *When they compliment you (or your company).* Compliments can be embarrassing, but shrugging off customers' sincere praise says, "You dummy, I'm not really that good." Instead, accept it gracefully, say thank you, and add, "I really appreciate your business."

3. *When they offer comments or suggestions.* Thanking customers for feedback says that you've heard what they had to say and value their opinion. Something as simple as, "Thank you for taking the time to tell me that! It really helps us know where we can do better," delivered with eye contact and a smile, can work wonders.

4. *When they try a new product or service.* Trying something new can make customers feel uncomfortable. Uncomfortable and risky. After all, the old and familiar is so, well, old and familiar. Thank customers for daring to try something different.

5. *When they recommend you to a friend.* When customers recommend you, they put themselves on the line. If you deliver, they look good. A written thank-you for a recommendation or a value-added token the next time you see those customers says you value their recommendation.

6. *When they are patient—and not so patient.* Whether they tell you about it or not (and, boy, will some customers tell you about it!), no one likes to wait. Thanking customers for their patience says you noticed and value their time. It's also one of the quickest ways to defuse customers who have waited too long.

7. *When they help you to serve them better.* Some customers are always prepared. They have their account numbers right at their fingertips, always bring the right forms, and kept notes on their last service call. They make your life a lot easier; thank them for it.

8. *When they complain to you.* Thank them for complaining? Absolutely! Customers who tell you they are unhappy are giving you a second chance. And that's quite a gift. Now you have a chance to win their renewed loyalty, which will give you additional opportunities to thank them in the future.

9. *When they make you smile.* A smile is one of the greatest gifts you can receive. Saying thank you just makes it better.

PART B

Thank-you Log			
A. People to Thank	**B. Why I'm Thanking Person**	**C. How I Will Express Thanks**	**D. Target Date**

ACTIVITY **75**

Making "Thank You" Personal

When it comes to thank-you's, there are opportunities you just shouldn't miss. Take this creative challenge to build sincere thank-you's for the different times you should show your appreciation.

PURPOSE:

✓ To create a sincere thank-you format that can be used by everyone to show appreciation for customers

✓ To discuss how to incorporate the "thank you" into daily interactions with customers

TIME: 20 minutes

DIRECTIONS:

1. Ask participants to form small groups. Explain that the purpose of Activity 75 is to establish times when they can repeatedly and consistently say "thank you" to their customers.

2. Have participants identify regular opportunities in their work when a "thank you" to customers might be appropriate and have an impact. Examples include when an order is placed, a confirmation is sent, a sale is completed, a compliment is offered, a suggestion is given, a complaint is filed, a wait time is too long, when customers try something new or different, when they make a referral that pans out, when someone does you a favor, when a vendor adds an extra feature. Be sure to record the suggestions on chart paper or white board.

3. Remind participants of the three ways to say thank you—verbally, in writing, or with a gift. Tell participants that you are going to focus on the written piece.

4. In their small groups, ask them to select one of the thank-you suggestions and create both a thank-you card and an e-mail that might be sent to a customer. Allow 10 minutes.

5. Have each group present their thank-you's.

6. Ask participants how these thank-you's will work for their internal partners. Discuss a time frame for including more thank-you's in their work processes.

ACTIVITY **76**

Thank-You Round Robin

It's not always easy to find the best way to say "thank you." The most effective thank-you's are immediate, specific, sincere, and special. Accepting a thank-you can be hard, too. This activity provides practice in both giving and receiving thanks.

PURPOSE:

✓ To be able to give sincere and specific thank-you's

✓ To practice saying and receiving a thank-you

TIME: 20 minutes

DIRECTIONS:

1. Explain to participants the purpose of Activity 76: that while it can be difficult to say "thank you" in the workplace, there is nothing more powerful for co-worker morale or customer delight.

2. Ask participants to select a partner to work with. Distribute copies of Activity 76 and ask participants to take a few minutes to prepare responses to the assignment. Allow 3 to 5 minutes.

3. Have participants take turns saying and accepting the thank-you's they have prepared. Allow 7 or 8 minutes for this exchange.

4. Use the following questions to debrief:
    * How did it make you feel to say "thank you"?
    * As you went along, did it get easier or harder?

- What was hard about accepting the thank-you?

- How might this exercise help you in using more thank-you's in your work with both external customers and internal partners?

5. Ask participants to make an effort to say "thank you" during the next week. They should keep either a written or a mental log of how it felt, how the person responded, and whether or not it got easier to do.

Practice both giving and receiving thank-you's.

1. What is something specific you can thank your partner for? (Examples: extra work, handling a customer well, attention to detail, patience explaining something, being there every day, bringing in a treat, offering to help someone).

_____

_____

_____

2. Pretending your partner is a customer, what have you experienced recently that might cause you to say "thank you"? (Examples: placed an order, called in with a good question, called your attention to a problem, paid you a compliment, made a useful complaint)

_____

_____

_____

3.   If your partner is your boss, what might you say "thank you" for? (Examples: giving you helpful information, running interference from higher management, offering you a special work assignment, providing you feedback for improvement, being there to answer questions, allowing you to attend a special meeting or training)

_____

_____

_____

4.   Pretend your partner is an internal customer, or someone you need for information, support, or to help an external customer. What might you say "thank you" for? (Examples: taking a transferred call and helping your customer, giving you important information, helping you understand a confusing situation, teaching you something about what they do, offering a suggestion for improvement, building your relationship)

_____

_____

_____

5.   Now, pretend you partner is you! How might you thank yourself? (Examples: for supporting a co-worker, for offering a suggestion for improvement, for going the extra mile for a customer, for being there every day, for doing the work you do, for solving a problem, for learning something new, for trying something new, for teaching someone)

_____

_____

_____

SECTION FOUR

The Problem-Solving Side of *Knock Your Socks Off Service*

How we "recover" when things go wrong for customers is the litmus test of service quality, separating the professionals from the amateurs in customer care. When the customer's Web-ordered product arrives in the wrong size or with missing parts, when the credit card company incorrectly charges a late fee, or when a restaurant meal is overcooked, the actions we take to soothe the customer and fix the problem determine whether those customers ever return.

But good service recovery isn't only about having a kind heart or remaining calm in the face of customer meltdowns. It's a product of well-conceived policies and procedures that empower employees to fit the right solution to the right problem for the right customer. It starts with acknowledging the customer's pain and apologizing for any distress, then moves quickly into finding a "fair fix" for a problem and offering some atonement for the inconvenience, and concludes with follow-up to ensure that the situation doesn't recur.

Service recovery requires the kind of sound judgment that enables service professionals to do what's right for aggrieved customers, yet not go overboard or give away the store. Such decision-making skill doesn't develop overnight. But with the support of guidelines that allow for flexibility within defined parameters and with the right training and experience, service workers can begin to make recovery decisions that create customers who become even more loyal to the organization than had they experienced no problem at all.

Knock Your Socks Off Service pros also recover well regardless of the setting, from disgruntled customers who approach them on the sales floor, to fire-breathing clients who phone call centers, to customers who send flaming-hot e-mails. Handling service breakdowns in these tense scenarios requires a different subset of recovery skills. As Rudyard Kipling said, "If you can keep your head when all those around you are losing theirs," you are well on the way to success. When we can show customers that we care about the pain or inconvenience they've experienced, we send a message that the company has their best interests at heart. That message helps bond those customers to the organization.

The activities in this section will give your service team the fortitude and skills to deal effectively with upset customers. They will provide a proven process for transforming unhappy campers into devoted followers.

The Service Recovery Process

The winners among service companies manage the design and deployment of service with a laser-like focus on the details. That means they work as hard at recovery after things go wrong for customers as they do at ensuring things go well the first time.

Recovery is the word we use to describe the effort to return a "broken" customer relationship to good health. Like medical recovery, healing a customer's negative perception of service requires direct and determined effort. Recover well, and aggrieved customers will be even more loyal to your organization than if they had not experienced a problem in the first place. The Service Recovery Process is a step-by-step means for restoring upset customers to an emotional balance.

PURPOSE:

✓ To observe the Service Recovery Process in action

✓ To relate the Service Recovery Process to your department or unit

✓ To build a plan to incorporate Service Recovery into daily work

TIME: 25 minutes

DIRECTIONS:

1. Review the Service Recovery Process chart in Part A of Activity 77. Discuss the steps with participants and talk about how you currently handle customers who have had service breakdowns in your company.

2. Show participants the "No Room at the Inn" video clip available on the amacombooks.org Web site.

3. As the group views the video, have them use Part B of Activity 77 to take notes on how each step of the Service Recovery Process was demonstrated. Also, they should consider how the customer responded during each step (e.g., reactions, attitudes, emotions).

4. Lead the group in a discussion of what they learned about the Service Recovery Process and how your organization can incorporate these lessons into its own recovery practices.

PART A

Service Recovery Process

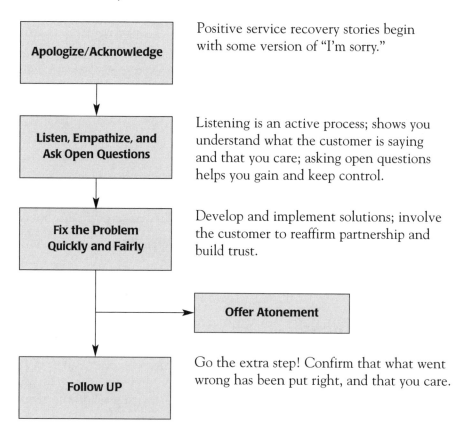

Apologize/Acknowledge

Positive service recovery stories begin with some version of "I'm sorry."

Listen, Empathize, and Ask Open Questions

Listening is an active process; shows you understand what the customer is saying and that you care; asking open questions helps you gain and keep control.

Fix the Problem Quickly and Fairly

Develop and implement solutions; involve the customer to reaffirm partnership and build trust.

Offer Atonement

Follow UP

Go the extra step! Confirm that what went wrong has been put right, and that you care.

Keep Your Promises. Customer expectations—stated or unstated, reasonable or unreasonable—form a promise between you and your customer. Be realistic about when and what you can and can't deliver.

Remember that each episode of a service breakdown is different. Sometimes you will need to use all the service recovery steps and at other times only a few. How you apply the Service Recovery Process will depend on the emotions of your customer and on the specifics of the situation. Only you are in a position to evaluate and act.

PART B

Identify how each phase of the Service Recovery Process is demonstrated in this situation. Take note of who initiates each component of the Recovery Process and how the other person responds.

1. Apologize _____

2. Listen, empathize, and ask open questions _____

3. Solve the problem quickly and fairly _____

4. Offer atonement _____

5. Keep your promises _____

6. Follow up _____

How might this process become part of the everyday service you provide?

_____

_____

_____

What might your department do to be better prepared for effective service recovery?

_____

_____

_____

ACTIVITY **78**

How Ready Are You to Recover?

One of the most effective tools for gauging the quality of recovery skills in your department or organization is to have everyone take a Recovery Skills Assessment. This is an opportunity to be as frank and honest as possible about how your group falls short in dealing with unhappy customers. At the same time, it is important to give credit where it is due, acknowledging ways in which your department shines in handling complaints.

PURPOSE:

✓ To evaluate individual and corporate responses to service recovery

✓ To identify individual and corporate strengths and weaknesses in service recovery

✓ To provide awareness of factors that contribute to extraordinary customer service experiences

TIME: 30 minutes

DIRECTIONS:

1. Have the participants individually complete the assessment in Part A of Activity 78. Assure them that their responses are confidential and so they should be completely honest.

2. Participants should use the Scoring Master (Part B of Activity 78) to calculate their scores, then total the scores to determine their overall result.

3. Ask for participants to identify the following:

- Areas in which they believe they and the company are strongest
- Areas in which they believe significant improvements can be made
- Results of the assessments that surprised them

4. Have participants agree to take the assessment again in three months, to determine if improvements have been made.

PART A

Systems, Policies, and Procedures

Choose yes or no to indicate the extent to which our systems, policies, and procedures make it easy for frontline and support employees to deliver quality service in the face of a service breakdown, and the degree to which systems, policies, and procedures are seen to support, rather than inhibit, good service recovery.

1. Assisting customers with problems is a clear priority in our company.

   ❏ YES   ❏ NO

2. The way my department/unit/division is organized makes it easy for employees to solve customer problems quickly.

   ❏ YES   ❏ NO

3. The way we are organized makes it easy for customers to reach the right individual or area when they have a problem or question.

   ❏ YES   ❏ NO

4. We provide a "service guarantee" to customers; it is well known among our customers.

   ❏ YES   ❏ NO

5. My department/unit/division has clear procedures for what to do when mistakes are made or errors are discovered.

   ❏ YES   ❏ NO

6. Customers experiencing problems can start the recovery process with a single contact; our procedures don't require customers to make multiple contacts to report a problem or get action.

    ❏ YES   ❏ NO

7. When problem solving takes longer than the initial contact, we have a system in place for staying in touch with the customer and updating him or her on the progress being made.

    ❏ YES   ❏ NO

8. Frontline employees are allowed to make value-added atonement gestures—such as "comping" a repair or extending a subscription— at their own discretion.

    ❏ YES   ❏ NO

9. All frontline and support employees know what they personally can do to solve customer problems.

    ❏ YES   ❏ NO

10. When a customer's problem is corrected, I am confident that it will not reoccur—at least for this customer.

    ❏ YES   ❏ NO

11. We have a formal process for collecting data on errors, complaints, and comments, for analyzing their significance, and for modifying our systems accordingly.

    ❏ YES   ❏ NO

Score (see Part B): _____

Improvements our department needs to make:_____

_____

_____

_____

Evaluating Service Performance

Choose yes or no (or otherwise correct answer) to reflect the degree to which we have established clear, customer-focused standards for service recovery, and the extent to which we measure quality of work performance against those standards.

1. My department/unit/division has set clear standards for response time to customer complaints, questions, inquiries, and other contacts and correspondence.

   ❑ YES   ❑ NO

2. Our standards are based on customer input rather than on internally generated technical criteria.

   ❑ YES   ❑ NO

3. We post our performance-to-standards data on a regular basis.

   ❑ YES   ❑ NO

4. For us, "regular" (from question 3 above) means:

   ❑ Daily   ❑ Weekly   ❑ Monthly

   ❑ Quarterly   ❑ Not at all

5. My department/unit/division meets or exceeds those standards on a regular basis.

   ❑ YES   ❑ NO

6. Our standards reflect "customer fixing" activities and outcomes as well as "problem fixing" activities and outcomes.

   ❑ YES   ❑ NO

7. We ask customers to evaluate us on the results of every service recovery effort.

   ❑ YES   ❑ NO

8. Customer evaluations include some elements of the following: reliability, assurance, tangibles, empathy, and responsiveness.

   ❑ YES   ❑ NO

9. We "shop" and/or do "ride alongs" with field representatives on a regular basis (at least twice a year).

   ❏ YES   ❏ NO

10. Some of our standards are tailored to specific customers with unique requirements.

    ❏ YES   ❏ NO

Score (see Part B): _____

Improvements we need to make:_____

_____

_____

_____

Customer Focus and Commitment
Choose yes or no to indicate the degree to which we as an organization, and each individual, thinks about, focuses on, and is concerned with satisfying our customers on a day-to-day basis.

1. I feel empowered to take action to resolve unusual customer needs or problems without requesting special permission.

   ❏ YES   ❏ NO

2. I feel a personal sense of pride and ownership when I use their service recovery skills to help customers.

   ❏ YES   ❏ NO

3. I am are not afraid to ask customers about their satisfaction with our products and services.

   ❏ YES   ❏ NO

4. We make a policy of asking customers what they expect from us when problems occur.

   ❏ YES   ❏ NO

5. Our current standards are a result of asking customers what they expect of us when problems occur.

   ❏ YES　　　　❏ NO .

6. There is good teamwork in my department/unit/division applied to solving customer problems.

   ❏ YES　　　　❏ NO

7. We almost always follow up with customers to ensure that their fixed problems stay fixed.

   ❏ YES　　　　❏ NO

8. It is not unusual to spot and resolve potential customer problems before the customer is aware of them.

   ❏ YES　　　　❏ NO

9. Everyone in my organization understands that retaining current customers through effective problem solving is as important as gaining new customers.

   ❏ YES　　　　❏ NO

10. Everyone in my part of the organization knows the "dollars and sense" of customer retention.

    ❏ YES　　　　❏ NO

Score (see Part B): _____

Improvements we need to make in these areas:_____

_____

_____

_____

Recognizing and Rewarding Service

Choose yes or no to reflect the degree to which individual and group efforts to prevent, spot, and solve customer problems are recognized and rewarded in your department/unit/division.

1. Managers and supervisors in my department/unit/division constantly look for evidence of employees taking a personal interest in resolving customer complaints and problems.

    ❑ YES   ❑ NO

2. Such employees are frequently "spot rewarded" in a tangible way for their efforts.

    ❑ YES   ❑ NO

3. Employees who practice good service recovery are held up as role models for other employees.

    ❑ YES   ❑ NO

4. Employees who make mistakes when working on behalf of a customer are confident that they will not be punished.

    ❑ YES   ❑ NO

5. Employees know that their ability to prevent, spot, and solve customer problems plays an important part in their performance reviews and decisions about advancement.

    ❑ YES   ❑ NO

6. We have a formal system that allows employees to recognize and thank other employees for their assistance in solving customers' problems.

    ❑ YES   ❑ NO

7. We have a formal system that encourages our customers to recognize employees for their assistance in preventing or correcting a service breakdown.

    ❑ YES   ❑ NO

Score (see Part B): _____

Improvements I need to make in these areas:_____

_____

_____

_____

Training and Coaching

Choose yes or no to indicate the degree to which I am trained and coached to do what is necessary to meet customers' needs and solve customers' problems.

1. I am encouraged to go above and beyond for customers.

    ❏ YES   ❏ NO

2. I believe that my above-and-beyond efforts for customers are recognized and valued.

    ❏ YES   ❏ NO

3. I am trained in the how-to's of:

    a. Listening carefully and fully to customers

        ❏ YES   ❏ NO

    b. "Reading" customer types and/or moods

        ❏ YES   ❏ NO

    c. Making positive impressions during problem fixing

        ❏ YES   ❏ NO

    d. Dealing with angry customers

        ❏ YES   ❏ NO

4. My department/unit/division takes specific actions to help employees deal with the stress that comes with customer contact.

   ❏ YES   ❏ NO

5. When I do not feel capable of dealing with a particular customer or a customer problem, I know whom to ask for assistance.

   ❏ YES   ❏ NO

6. Managers and supervisors in my department/unit/division regularly meet one-on-one with employees to coach them on service recovery skills.

   ❏ YES   ❏ NO

7. Employees regularly meet together—without a manager present—to discuss tough customer problems and to exchange information on solving customer problems.

   ❏ YES   ❏ NO

Score (see Part B): _____

Improvements I need to make in these areas:_____

_____

_____

_____

PART B

How ready are we to recover when things go wrong for customers?

Scoring Master				
Systems, Policies, and Procedures	**Evaluating Service Performance**	**Customer Focus and Commitment**	**Recognizing and Rewarding Service**	**Train and Coach**
1. 2 0	1. 3 0	1. 3 0	1. 2 0	1. 3 0
2. 3 0	2. 2 0	2. 2 0	2. 2 0	2. 2
3. 3 0	3. 2 0	3. 2 0	3. 2 0	3. a = 2, b = 1 c = 2, d = 3 Max = 8
4. 2 0	4. 2 for D/M/W 1 for Q	4. 3 0	4. 2 0	4. 2 0
5. 3 0	5. 3 0	5. 2 0	5. 3 0	5. 2 0
6. 2 0	6. 2 0	6. 3 0	6. 2 0	6. 2 0
7. 2 0	7. 2 for Every 1 for Month	7. 2 0	7. 2 0	7. 2 0
8. 2 0	8. 2 for all 5 1 for 3 of 5	8. 2 0		
9. 2 0	9. 2 0	9. 1 0		
10. 3 0	10. 3 0	10. 1 0		
11. 2 0				
Total 26 0	**Total 21 0**	**Total 21 0**	**Total 15 0**	**Total 21 0**
Minimum Comfort Zone: 20	Minimum Comfort Zone: 16	Minimum Comfort Zone: 16	Minimum Comfort Zone: 12	Minimum Comfort Zone: 12

Recovery report card:

91–104: A+; 85–90: A; 80–84: B+; 75–79: B

Less than 79 points: Not any worse than anybody else—and not any better.

Using the Well-Placed "I'm Sorry"

The words are so simple—"I'm sorry"—yet we hear them far too infrequently from service providers. Our research shows that when customers tell a company about a problem with a product or service, they receive an apology less than half the time. The solution to every problem, whether major or minor, should start with a sincere apology. This isn't an acknowledgment of fault but, rather, a show of empathy for the difficulties customers have experienced, regardless of the cause.

PURPOSE:

✓ To learn the real meaning of an apology

✓ To recognize why it is hard to apologize

✓ To write sample apologies for use in the future

TIME: 20 minutes (This exercise works well in conjunction with Activity 77.)

DIRECTIONS:

1. If you have already reviewed the Service Recovery Process (Activity 77), it is probably safe to jump to this activity. If you have not covered it, be sure to put the concept of this activity into context by linking it with the Service Recovery Process.

2. Ask participants the following questions to get them thinking about the nature of an apology:

- What is important about making an apology to a customer? (It is a way of acknowledging that the customer's upset and let's him or her know we are listening.)

- When we apologize, who "owns" the problem? (No one really "owns" the problem; but the apology is an acknowledgment that a problem has developed and the customer has experienced some pain.)

- What gets in the way of our offering the customer an apology? (Saying we're sorry means we "own" the problem; it suggests that we caused or created the problem, even if we know the customer was the source; the company's legal department may frown on the apology as an admission of blame; some other department may have caused the problem and now we have to deal with it [scapegoating]; it's hard for people to say they are sorry; it doesn't sound sincere to the customer—because we're not sorry.)

3. Distribute copies of Activity 79. In small groups, have participants write generic apologies that will fit the most common situations they face daily.

4. Ask each group to offer one apology they have written. Ask the other participants how they would react to the apology they heard. Have groups revise as necessary.

5. Ask for a volunteer to collect the pages, compile the results, and reproduce the summary for distribution. Then, encourage participants to use these apologies in the next week and keep track of the reactions or responses that the customers give. Agree to review customer reactions and responses and what participants learn at the next meeting.

Apology Worksheet

Situations That Frequently Require an Apology	Sample Apology

Finding the Right Fix

Customers have high expectations for service recovery, just as they have high expectations for normal service. Some of those expectations are easy to figure out; others are more subtle. Certainly they want you to fix their problems. But what kind of fix will make each of them happy? And how can you fix the problem without busting the department's budget?

PURPOSE:

 To discuss customer expectations for problem resolution

✓ To agree on the range of options for resolving common customer problems

TIME: 20 minutes (Consider combining this with Activity 79 for greater impact.)

DIRECTIONS:

1. Ask participants to think of a situation when they had a problem with a product or service and had to go back to the provider or voice their complaint on the spot. Ask them to think specifically about what they wanted to have happen as a result. Then, ask two or three participants to offer examples.

2. Point out that people have unique expectations for how their service providers should handle their situations. Remind the group that there is no one-size-fits-all recovery solution for service breakdowns.

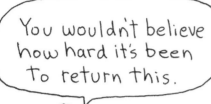

3. Have participants form small groups of three or four each. Distribute copies of Activity 80 and ask them to spend the next 7 to 8 minutes together completing the form.

4. Ask each group to present its answers. Point out that they will all receive copies of the group's responses following the meeting. As you hear from each group, be sure to point out when different suggestions for meeting customer expectations are identified and varying resolutions have been offered.

5. At the conclusion of the meeting, ask for a volunteer to collect the worksheets, compile the results, and make photocopies for the whole group.

Finding the Right Fix Analysis		
Problem	**Customer Expectation**	**Resolutions**
If the customer problem is…	And the customer expects…	I can…

Putting Recovery Knowledge into Action

All service providers encounter customers who have been disappointed by some aspect of the service or product offered. But it's important to view this disappointment as a great opportunity to make that person a loyal customer—if we can resolve the problem with the proper dose of empathy and efficiency.

PURPOSE:

✓ To apply the Service Recovery Process to real-world situations

✓ To identify areas of service recovery where personal improvement can be made

TIME: 20 minutes (This activity could be paired with Activity 77.)

DIRECTIONS:

1. Review Activity 77 before beginning Activity 81.

2. Distribute the Service Recovery Analysis sheet (Activity 81) and have participants identify a recent or current Service Recovery problem. Direct them to complete the column marked "What I Did" first. Then move on to the next column. Once completed, ask participants to analyze any differences.

3. Use the following questions to debrief the participants after they have completed the form:

• What steps were missing in your original interaction?

Service Recovery Analysis

- What improvements did you identify as you reworked this example?

- What types of follow-up actions did you include?

- How will you apply the Service Recovery Process in your work every day?

Describe a complaint you recently received from a customer. (internal or external):

_____

_____

_____

_____

_____

_____

_____

_____

Using the Service Recovery Process model, record the steps you took to resolve the customer's problem. Identify ways you might handle this type of situation differently in the future.

Step	What I Did	What I Could Do Differently in the Future
Acknowledge/Empathize/ Ask: • Apologize • Show empathy • Listen actively • Ask open-ended questions • Be sincere		
Fix the problem: • Develop and implement a solution • Involve the customer in the solution		
Offer atonement • Offer a gesture of goodwill		
Follow up: • Internally • With the customer • With the organization/ your manager		

ACTIVITY **82**

Tell Me a Story

Sharing personal stories and experiences among service providers is one of the best teaching tools there is. Everyone picks up little hints, tips, and techniques in hearing other people's stories and these hints and techniques can easily be incorporated into our own behaviors at work.

PURPOSE:

✓ To use a training environment to explore how others have handled difficult customer situations

✓ To discuss options for handling common problem scenarios

✓ To identify actions that lead to Memory Makers for disgruntled customers

TIME: 30 minutes

DIRECTIONS:

1. Break the participants into groups of three to five people each.

2. Have each participant in a group tell a story of a recovery situation, either as a service provider or as a customer. Give each participant 2 to 3 minutes to share her or his story with the rest of their group. Instruct the other people in the groups to list the positive behaviors that were described. For example, did the service provider apologize? Did the provider ask open-ended questions? Follow up? Fix the problem? Involve the customer?

3. With the large group reassembled, have participants briefly recount the experiences they heard about, listing all the positive recovery behaviors that were in evidence. List these on a chart paper or white board for the group to see.

4. Distribute copies of Activity 82—the list of Memory Makers. These are actions that transform potentially bad memories into positive ones for customers in the aftermath of service problems. Ask participants the following questions:

   • How does the list on the board compare to the list of Memory Makers?

   • What is the focus of these Memory Makers? (fixing the person)

   • What is missing from the list of Memory Makers? (fixing the problem)

   • How might we change the way customers' problems are resolved to sharpen the focus on the Memory Makers?

Service Recovery Memory Makers

These Memory Makers were items captured from more than 90 focus groups conducted by Performance Research Associates. Participants represented customers of retail and hospitality businesses, professional services, business-to-business services, transportation, logistics, and manufacturing. The percentages indicate the frequency with which these participants noted that the service provider demonstrated that behavior during the recovery process.

Dealt with customer's emotional state	79.0%
Apologized	69.1%
Showed humility/poise	62.9%
Followed up afterwards	56.8%
Showed problem-solving skill	53.0%
Admitted organizational error, when appropriate	44.4%
Acted fully empowered	40.7%
Showed good listening	40.7%
Showed empathy	38.3%
Acted with urgency	35.8%
Created value added	32.1%
Believed the customer	24.7%

ACTIVITY **83**

Make Customers Your Partners in Problem Solving

Customers who are asked to participate in a problem-solving effort are more satisfied with the resolution than those who aren't asked. Critical to creating a sense of partnership is the way you invite the customer into the problem solving process.

PURPOSE:

✓ To experience the value of a problem-solving partnership with customers

✓ To prepare ways to invite customers to join the partnership

TIME: 30–40 minutes

DIRECTIONS:

1. Divide participants into an even number of teams, preferably with no teams larger than four participants.

2. Explain the rules for solving the puzzle. During the first round, some teams will solve a Sudoku puzzle jointly, while members of other teams will solve it as individuals. For groups solving the puzzle as a team, distribute only one copy of Part A of Activity 83 per team. For those working individually, distribute a copy to each participant.

3. During the second round, the teams and the individuals solve another Sudoku puzzle, reversing the tasks—those who worked individually now team up, while those who worked as teams now work individually.

4. Instruct the participants that they will have 5 minutes to complete their puzzles in each round. Part B contains the solutions to both puzzles.

5. Reassemble the group and ask the following questions:

- Was your reaction to working alone different from your reaction to working in a team?

- Why do you think people have different reactions to working alone and working in a team?

- What might cause some people to prefer teamwork to independent work? Why would others have the opposite preference?

- What are the advantages of teamwork? What are the advantages of independent work?

- If you are an expert Sudoku puzzler, how did you feel about working in a team? About working alone?

- Now, let's think about our customers. What can we do to include them in some of the complex situations we encounter?

- What situations do we need to continue to work alone?

PART A

Individual Sudoku Puzzle

1. Fill the empty squares of the grid using the numbers 1, 2, 3, 4, 5, and 6.

2. Each of the six numbers should appear only once in:

- Each row (six horizontal squares from left to right)

- Each column (six vertical squares from top to bottom)

- Each block (the 2 × 3 rectangles surrounded by thick lines)

6		4		5	2
	5				
3	4		5		1
5		1		4	3
	1	3		6	
2	6		3		4

Team Sudoku Puzzle

1. Fill the empty squares of the grid using the numbers 1, 2, 3, 4, 5, and 6.

2. Each of the six numbers should appear only once in:
   - Each row (six horizontal squares from left to right)
   - Each column (six vertical squares from top to bottom)
   - Each block (the 2 × 3 rectangles surrounded by thick lines)

			4	3	1
4	1		5	6	
1			3	2	6
3	6	2			4
	3	1		4	5
2	5	4	6	1	3

PART B

Answer for Individual Puzzle

6	3	4	1	5	2
1	5	2	4	3	6
3	4	6	5	2	1
5	2	1	6	4	3
4	1	3	2	6	5
2	6	5	3	1	4

Answer for Team Puzzle

5	2	6	4	3	1
4	1	3	5	6	2
1	4	5	3	3	6
3	6	2	1	5	4
6	3	1	2	4	5
2	5	4	6	1	3

ACTIVITY **84**

Maximize Your Web Site Impact

More and more customers are shopping online, and when they have feedback to offer on how easy (or challenging) it is to use your company Web site to order products or find out about your services, frontline service professionals are often the first to receive it. That positions these associates as key listening posts, able to collect valuable customer input on Web site design and usability that can be passed on to the information technology department.

PURPOSE:

✓ To raise participants' awareness of their value as key frontline "listening posts"

✓ To stress the importance of cross-functional communications and information-sharing in improving service quality

✓ To give participants more insight into the customer's buying experience

TIME: 3 weeks

DIRECTIONS:

1. Explain to participants that the goal of this activity is to track and collect, for a three-week period, any comments they receive from customers regarding the design or user-friendliness of the company's Web site.

2. If time permits following regular service interactions, suggest that service professionals be proactive and pose a question of their own to customers:

- Have you used our Web site in the past few months?
- If yes, what was your impression of the site?
- Did you encounter any difficulties or challenges in its use?
- Would you like to see any improvements?

3. Distribute copies of the Web Site Log Sheet of Activity 84. Stress that associates should categorize the feedback as follows:

   - *Easy access to a toll free number.* Can customers easily find a toll free number on the Web site if they need help from a live service rep?
   - *E-mail response and instant chat.* If customers recently communicated with the company by e-mail, were they happy with the speed of response? The quality of the answer? If they have used instant chat, did it prove to be a valuable service?
   - *Search function.* Did the search function narrow a search for a customer to make it easier to find product or service information?
   - *FAQ.* Was the list of Frequently Asked Questions thorough, and were answers easy to understand?
   - *Overall site design.* Was design of the site clear, was the site easy to navigate, and was it visually appealing?
   - *Product ordering process.* Was it easy for customers to find relevant information for products they were looking for (price, size, and other key specifications?) and then move quickly through the check-out process?
   - *Return policies.* If customers have had to return a product ordered from the Web site, did they find the process easy to use and customer friendly?

4. At the end of the three-week process, have associates summarize the feedback and write a brief report (one to two pages) of key findings. Collect those findings and present them to the Web design function in your information technology group.

5. Thank the participants for their extra work (consider handing out a small token of appreciation) and remind them how valuable their eyes and ears can be to other departments in the organization. Because of their daily contact with customers on the frontlines, they likely know more about customer likes and dislikes than anyone else in the company, and that information can be a gold mine for improving service quality.

Web Site Log Sheet

- Have you used our web site in the past few months?

- If yes, what was your impression of the site?

- Did you encounter any difficulties or challenges in its use?

- Would you like to see any improvements?

Track the number of comments you hear regarding each topic. Use the comment page that follows to provide more detail.

	Week 1	Week 2	Week 3
Access to toll-free #			
E-mail response and instant chat			
Search function			
FAQ			
Overall site design			
Ordering process			
Return policies			

Record the specific comments you have received from customers regarding the Web site.

_____

_____

_____

Matching Atonement to the Error

It's a truism of service recovery that while all customers who experience problems are worthy of fair and respectful treatment, some receive higher levels of recovery simply because of the greater value they bring to the organization. Atonement must fit the error—and the customer.

PURPOSE:

 To recognize that service recovery isn't a one-size-fits-all proposition

 To consider different atonement options for different situations

 To reinforce that, even though atonement may be tailored to the customer, care and respect are given to all customers

TIME: 20 minutes (This activity pairs nicely with Activity 31.)

DIRECTIONS:

1. Ask participants to provide examples of a problem situation they encountered involving a high-value customer and requiring an escalated level of organizational resources or effort. Additionally, ask them for examples of problem scenarios involving less-valued customers. What might be the appropriate atonements for these situations?

2. Divide participants into four groups, and distribute copies of Part A of Activity 85. NOTE: Suggested answers may be found in Part B of the activity.

3. Direct the teams to read the Southern Express case. Assign one customer situation to each group, and explain that they should consider the following for their customer:

- The level or type of customer and the specifics of the situation.
- The level of service recovery effort to be expended and the actions to be taken, and why.

4. Reassemble the group and ask the teams to present the highlights of their discussions about their customers. Invite others to add to each presentation, as time permits. Emphasize that while problems should be resolved for all customers, service providers need to also tailor their recovery resources and efforts to the type of customer and the specifics of the situation.

5. Use the following questions to expand the discussion of this activity to more general department practices:

- What forms of atonement might we offer our customers?
- What's your comfort level in offering atonement?
- What typical problems do you face in dealing with different kinds of customers?
- What types of atonement might you offer a customer in each of these situations?
- When is it appropriate to offer a gesture of atonement?
- What levels of atonement are you authorized to offer?
- How do you handle a customer who is not satisfied with your offer?
- When might you need to contact a supervisor to authorize a value-added gesture for a customer?

PART A
The Southern Express Case

You are the manager of the Customer Inquiry Division of Southern Express, a large credit card company. Your division is made up largely of call-center operators who respond to customer problems, questions, and complaints. You believe that frontline operators who can effectively handle service recovery would offer a key strategic advantage over your competition. To accomplish this goal, you set guidelines and parameters for handling different types of customers under different circumstances. When a customer calls, the service representatives input the customer's name and the computer screen shows the type of Southern Express card holder who is on the line, plus his or her present account status.

The following are levels of card holders and their complaint call, with questions regarding the appropriate response and space to write your answers.

Platinum Card Holder

"I'm calling from the Neiman-Marcus store, ordering a set of mink headrests—they were going to be a present for my wife. When they ran my Southern Express card through their machine—I've been a member since '74—it was rejected! And when they called to check my account, your telephone number was busy. You can imagine how embarrassed I was when they kept the card and asked me to leave. Why, even my driver acted huffy toward me!"

1. What service recovery effort would be most effective and why?

   _____

2. Is atonement appropriate and, if yes, what would you offer?

   _____

Blue Card Holder 1

"You're not gonna believe what just happened! I'm at the local marina and was gassing up my boat to do some fishing. The attendant pumping the gas dropped my Southern Express card in a puddle of gasoline and the dang thing about melted. They can't get it to work and you can't read any of the numbers."

1. What service recovery effort would be most effective and why?

   _____

2. Is atonement appropriate and, if yes, what would you offer?

   _____

Blue Card Holder 2

"I'm here at the Sears store in the mall, trying to buy a new chain saw. The clerk refused to take my Southern Express card—said they'd only take a Sears, Discover, or MasterCard card. You need to call and set them straight."

1. What service recovery effort would be most effective and why?

   _____

2. Is atonement appropriate and, if yes, what would you offer?

   _____

Red Card Holder

"I'm calling from Billy Bob's Bar and Barbecue Basement, in Batesville. I whipped out my Southern Express card a while ago to pay for a couple of rounds, and the bartender said my card had expired. How come you never sent me a new card? I send money every three or four months! I'm not much on having to wash dishes to pay for a few beers!"

1. What service recovery effort would be most effective and why?

   _____

2. Is atonement appropriate and, if yes, what would you offer?

   _____

PART B
Suggested Answers

Platinum Card

"Sir, I'm very sorry this has happened—I can hear that you're very frustrated about this situation. I'm looking at your account and it shows that you've exceeded your limit. However, because you are one of our finest customers, it would be my pleasure to increase that for you right now. In fact, if Neiman-Marcus is still accessible, I'd be happy to talk with the person who was assisting you and get this cleared up for you."

Blue Card 1

"Wow—that doesn't sound good at all! Here's what I can do for you. Southern Express will be pleased to overnight a replacement card that you will have tomorrow. In the meantime, after you can verify a few security questions, I can give you your account number to use for any purchases you may need today. Additionally, let me make sure you have our 24-hour toll-free number so you may reach us right away should we be able to help you further."

Blue Card 2

"I'm very sorry this has happened. I'm sure it's put you in a very difficult situation. If you can give me your location, I can refer you to the nearest ATM that accepts the Southern Express card. You could then make your purchase with cash. Unfortunately, Southern Express can't control which organizations choose to take advantage of our services."

Red Card

"Oh, I'm sorry this has happened to you. Our records indicate that a new card was sent to you on February 7, and that it was activated from your home phone number on February 19. There have been no purchases made with the card. Is it possible it's still at home or that another member of your family is using the card? I am authorized to approve just this charge to your new account number. Any further charges will need to be verified with the security numbers from the new card."

Fix the Customer First, Then the Problem

The toughest part of dealing with people, as you already know, is dealing with people. When there is a problem, customers often take it out on the first person they talk to—regardless of whether it was you who caused the problem. It's tempting to respond in kind to the emotional fireworks. Tempting, but not very wise, and certainly not very productive. It's not enough to just fix the problem; you also have to "fix" the person.

PURPOSE:

✓ To recognize the different kinds of disgruntled customers

✓ To build a plan for dealing with each type of customer

✓ To create a departmental agreement to support each other in dealing with unhappy customers, should the need arise

TIME: 30 minutes

DIRECTIONS:

1. Distribute copies of Part A of Activity 86 and review the types of upset customers—Blasé Blue, Ornery Orange, Raging Red.

2. Distribute copies of Part B and use the situations provided, or create a problem scenario from your own work experience, to have participants decide how to handle each customer type. They should write down their responses in the spaces provided. Remind participants that it is

just as important to "fix" the person first—that is, to acknowledge the customer's unhappiness, to express empathy, and to ease the customer to a state of emotional balance—as it is to solve the problem. Once you've "fixed" the customers psychologically, you can directly solve their problems.

3. Working through one level of customer at a time, review the participants' responses, discussing their various approaches. Chart the responses to build a model for each level of customer. Again, it is critical in this exercise that participants "fix" the person first, then solve the problem. Listen for words and phrases like "empathy," "apology," "listening," "asking open-ended questions," "involving the customer."

4. Ask the participants how they might support each other when one of them has a Raging Red or high-level Ornery Orange customer to deal with. Again, chart their responses to build a "pact" that everyone in the department will follow.

5. Following the meeting, write up the results and distribute the agreement to participants.

PART A

Types of Upset Customers

- *Blasé Blue Customers.* These customers don't give you enough emotional clues to decipher their level of upset. For some, their service breakdown may simply be a nonemotional event—they roll with the punch and don't let it bother them. But be aware that seemingly neutral customers can move up the emotional scale if you don't take them seriously.

- *Ornery Orange Customers.* Annoyed, these people exhibit mild irritation because their customer experience has fallen short of their expectations. Take them lightly or refuse to acknowledge their unhappiness, however, and you can quickly escalate them to four-alarm fire status. Handle with care.

- *Raging Red Customers.* These customers have major feelings of ire and frustration; they feel victimized and hurt by the service breakdown. Usually you won't have any trouble identifying their level of concern—it will be obvious to everyone within a three-block radius.

PART B

To see the differences among these three customer types, consider these reactions to essentially the same initial situation: a late airplane flight. Each customer approaches you at the gate desk for assistance.

1. *Blasé Blue*. Bob's flight arrives one hour late, but he had a ninety-minute layover and can still make his next connection, so Bob's plans haven't been affected. He asks, "Even though I am late, I assume I can board the plane at any time since I hold Elite status."

    How would you work effectively with Bob?

    _____

    _____

2. *Ornery Orange*. Olivia's flight is one hour late, causing her to miss a connection and to have to rebook on a later flight. She attacks with, "I can't believe your airline. It's never on time. I just hope there is another flight I can get. Honestly, I've about had it with all of you."

    How would you work effectively with Olivia?

    _____

    _____

3. *Raging Red*. Ray's flight is one hour late, causing him to miss the day's last connection, resulting in an unplanned overnight stay and the need to call and reschedule a full day's worth of appointments. He shouts, "This is a complete outrage. I have never had to deal with such incompetence in my life. I don't think you get the whole grasp of this issue. I'm about to lose a huge deal and none of this is my fault. What are you going to do for me? How are you going to compensate me for my loss of time, income, and relationship with my client? Get me out of here!"

    How would you work effectively with Ray?

    _____

    _____

ACTIVITY **87**

Fix the Customer Role-Play

Customers, particularly upset customers, don't always explain the facts of their situation clearly or completely. "Fixing" the person—restoring her or him to a state of emotional balance—is as important to a well-executed recovery effort as is fixing the problem.

PURPOSE:

✓ To experience the difference between fixing just the problem and fixing both the person and the problem

✓ To practice using the soothing words and phrases that will work for you

TIME: 30 minutes

DIRECTIONS:

1. Ask participants to select a partner. Explain that they will be asked to role-play a situation in two different ways. In the first version, the focus should be on fixing only the problem. In the second role-play, the focus should be twofold: on fixing the person, then fixing the problem. Have the partners decide which of them will go first.

2. Distribute copies of Activity 87, detailing the scenarios. Ask teams to review the situations, plan their approach, then begin. Allow up to 4 minutes for the first role-play.

3. Call time and ask the customers to provide feedback to the service providers on how well the role-play worked—whether the service providers moved quickly and fairly to a solution, and whether the customer was involved in the process and felt valued.

4. Ask the teams to reverse the roles and use the second situation, this time with a focus on attending to the person first (dealing with the customer's emotional state), then resolving the problem. Again, allow up to 4 minutes for the role-play.

5. Call time and ask the customers to give feedback, focusing on how much attention was paid to attending to the customer first, then to solving the problem.

6. Reassemble the group to discuss the activity, using the following questions:

- What is the difference in feel and approach between the two situations?
- How did the customers respond to the service recovery approach each time?
- How were the responses different?
- How much additional time did it take to focus on the person and not just the problem?
- What have you learned from the role-play that you can take back to the workplace?

Fix the Customer Role-Play

Situation 1: Fix the Problem

A customer walks in the door and immediately approaches the service desk. The customer bangs down a boxed coffeemaker and immediately starts in with the following information, "Why is it that this place cannot get good-quality people to write the instructions for their products? I am an American. I read English. I am bright and can follow directions very well. But what is included in this box is nothing near English, readable, or understandable. What happened to good ol' American workers? Why can't you get the person who is responsible for this product to review the directions and make sure any reasonable English-speaking person can follow these directions?"

- *Service Provider.* As you work through this problem, focus on resolving the problem quickly and fairly. It is clear you have a good handle on the situation and know just how to resolve the problem to keep the customer happy. How will you resolve this situation for the customer—quickly and fairly?

- *Customer.* As the customer in this situation, you are very frustrated about the seemingly inadequate instructions included with this product. The focus of this role-play is to move to resolution of the problem immediately. Be resistant to a solution unless the service provider involves you in the problem-solving process. If that happens, agree to help and move to a solution quickly. When the problem is resolved, this does not eliminate your frustration.

Situation 2: Fix the Person, Then the Problem
See situation 1 above—same customer with the same complaint.

- *Service Provider.* As you work through this problem, focus on attending to the customer's emotional state first, before solving the problem. Remember to use Empathy statements. Listen attentively so you can detect the level of emotion and perhaps the underlying concern, then work toward resolution. How will you attend to the customer's emotional state prior to resolving the problem?

- *Customer.* The focus of this role-play is for the service provider to first neutralize your emotions, then resolve the problem. If the service provider moves to resolving the problem immediately, without acknowledging your feelings, you just get madder. Be resistant to a solution unless the service provider begins with an empathy statement, listens to what you say, and asks you some good open-ended questions. If that happens, agree to help and move to a solution quickly. If the service provider does a good job of neutralizing your emotions, express your gratitude for her or his help. If the service provider doesn't focus on you, before moving to problem resolution, say something like, "Why can't you just remember who your customers are and make it easy for us?" Or, "Just a minute there; I'm not finished yet." Then continue your tirade.

ACTIVITY **88**

Calming Obnoxious Customers

The key to effectively handling obnoxious customers is for service providers to avoid becoming caught up in their customers' emotions. When service providers stay professional, they put themselves in a position to help, creating a partnership between the customer and the organization.

PURPOSE:

✓ To master the four steps for dealing with obnoxious customers

✓ To apply the four techniques to real situations

✓ To remember the importance of remaining professional at all times

TIME: 15 minutes

DIRECTIONS:

1. Review with participants the four techniques listed in Part A of Activity 88. Ask where they may have questions or concerns about the techniques. Discuss as appropriate.

2. Distribute copies of Part B to the group and ask them to answer the questions.

3. In discussion, ask participants to provide examples for each strategy, based on their answers to the questions.

4. Together as a group, build a plan for the Transfer Transformation strategy that will work in the department. Chart ideas for everyone to see and review. The following questions may be helpful:

  - How do we currently support each other in difficult situations?
  - What might we use as a verbal cue that help is needed?
  - How might we process a transfer after the call is complete?

5. Ask for a volunteer to write up the agreed upon conclusions for distribution to all participants.

PART A

Four Steps to Dealing with Difficult Customers

1. *See no evil, hear no evil.* Resist the temptation to return the customer's fire. Treat the customer with courtesy and respect.

2. *Surface the tension.* Bring the feelings to the surface. Ask, "Have I personally done something to upset you? I'd like to help. Please give me a chance."

3. *Transfer Transformation.* Give the customer an adult "time out" by transferring him or her to one of your peers or to a supervisor.

4. *Build contractual trust.* Establish an agreement with the customer whereby you need the customer to stop a particular behavior in order to resolve the problem, and state what the consequences will be if the behavior continues.

PART B

1. Describe an encounter with an obnoxious customer that you have either experienced or witnessed.

_____

_____

_____

_____

2. What could you do in that situation to "See no evil, hear no evil"?

_____

_____

_____

_____

3. How will you "Surface the Tension"?

_____

_____

_____

_____

4. If you need to use the "Transfer Transformation" technique, to whom will you transfer the customer? Why?

_____

_____

_____

_____

5. If the customer becomes threatening or uses unacceptable behaviors, what kind of a contractual statement will you make?

_____

_____

_____

_____

This activity is available at: www.amacombooks.org/go/101ActDKYSOS
© 2009 AMACOM, a division of American Management Association.

Customers From Hell®
Hall of Shame

Not all Customers From Hell are created equal. Some are masters at beating the slow drum of criticism; others are top-of-their-lungs screamers. Some beg, some cry, some threaten. A few even flatter. Our advice is: Know the enemy!

PURPOSE:

✓ To identify the characteristics of each Customer From Hell

✓ To develop strategies for working with each archetype

✓ To have some fun role-playing each type of customer

TIME: 30 minutes

DIRECTIONS:

1. Distribute copies of Part A of Activity 89 and review with participants the descriptions of the five types of Customers From Hell.

2. Ask participants if they can recognize each of these customers in people they deal with on the job.

3. Generate a list of the best ways to interact with each customer type. (Note: This should generate some good discussion.)

4. Distribute copies of Part B of Activity 89 and compare the group's list with the suggestions provided.

5. Now, have some fun. Create examples of typical problems that customers experience in your business. Depending on the size of the group, either form small groups of three to five people each, or stay together as a whole. Ask for a volunteer to play the role of a Customer From Hell. Select a situation and have the remaining participants play the role of service provider. Role-play the situations while applying the techniques for dealing with these difficult customers. Work though each type of Customer From Hell, rotating the players in the "hellish" role.

PART A

Customers From Hell® Hall of Shame

- **Egocentric Edgar.** Me first, me last, me only—that's his creed. You? You're just a bit player, an extra, an extraneous piece of scenery in that grandest of all productions, *Edgar: The Greatest Story Ever Told.*

  Sample Behaviors. Won't wait his turn, will only speak to whoever is in charge, intimidates through judicious name dropping, and makes loud demands.

- **Bad-mouth Betty.** Her mother would be proud. Such an extensive vocabulary! It takes timing, talent, and a total lack of shame to swear like a trooper, but Betty makes it look easy.

  Sample Behaviors. Uses language and has a demeanor that is caustic, crude, cruel, and foul.

- **Hysterical Harold.** He's a screamer. If it's true that there is a child in all of us yearning to break free, Harold demonstrates the dark side of that happy thought. He is the classic tantrum-thrower, the adult embodiment of the terrible twos. Only louder, much louder.

  Sample Behaviors. Screams, is rabid and extremely animated, jumps around, and invades the personal space of others.

- **Dictatorial Dick.** Dick often shows up with marching orders. He issues ultimatums, sets arbitrary deadlines, and tells everyone exactly how to

This activity is available at: www.amacombooks.org/go/101ActDKYSOS
© 2009 AMACOM, a division of American Management Association.

do their jobs—after all, he "used to be in the business." And, when his plan doesn't work? It's your company's fault, of course.

Sample Behaviors. Shows up with multiple copies of written directions or orders, insists on doing things his way, and suspects sabotage if things don't go his way.

* **Freeloading Freda.** A material girl in a material world, she wants her dollar's worth—and yours, and mine, and anyone else's she can get. She doesn't make a game of getting more for her money; for her, it's a war.

Sample Behaviors. Wants something for nothing or, better yet, two for nothing; brings something back when it wears out, breaks, or begins to bore her, and screams lawsuit or slander if accused of taking advantage.

PART B

Egocentric Edgar

* *Appeal to his ego*—acknowledge him as a VIP, remember and use his name.

* *Demonstrate action*—take measurable, immediate action.

* *Don't talk policy*—say something like, "For you I can offer…" then offer whatever your standard policy is.

* *Don't let his ego destroy yours*—focus on the business at hand and don't take him personally.

Bad-Mouth Betty

* *Ignore her language*—try saying something like, "Excuse me, have I done something personally to offend you? If I have, I'd like to fix it or apologize."

* *Force the issue*—interrupt her and say, "Excuse me, but I don't have to listen to that kind of language and I'm going to hang up right now."

* *Use selective agreement*—agree with her if you can and acknowledge her complaint.

Hysterical Harold

- *Let him vent*—use an empathy statement to acknowledge his feelings and concern.

- *Take it backstage*—walk him to a more secluded area.

- *Take responsibility for solving the problem*—let him know that you want to and will do something to solve the problem.

Dictatorial Dick

- *Break up his game*—nothing works on Dick like fulfilling his request promptly and accurately.

- *Stick to your game*—accentuate the positive by repeating what you can do for him.

Freeloading Freda

- *Treat Freda with courtesy and respect*—just like any other customer.

- *Find a fair response to her complaint*—fair in your mind and hers.

- *You do not have to give in to her demands*—weigh that over the scene she may cause if you don't.

This activity is available at: www.amacombooks.org/go/101ActDKYSOS
© 2009 AMACOM, a division of American Management Association.

ACTIVITY **90**

Difficult Customer Match Game

There is a world of difference between keeping your composure while working with a mildly upset customer and allowing a fire-breathing, show-no-mercy, take-no-prisoners Customer From Hell to get you so upset you develop a burning sensation in your stomach.

PURPOSE:

✓ To recognize the difference between a Customer From Hell and one who has been through hell

✓ To have some fun while venting your feelings about difficult customers

TIME: 20 minutes (Activity 89 is prerequisite here.)

DIRECTIONS:

1. Remind participants that there are different species of upset customers. Probably 95 percent of those upset customers are just frustrated or angry that they have had to repeat their story for the third time, have been transferred to yet another department, or have had to put out an all-points bulletin to find a live service rep. We refer to these people as customers who have been through hell. The remaining 5 percent are those impossible and irrational customers who just never seem to be satisfied, regardless of what you do, and whose nasty emotional states appear to be almost congenital. We call this latter group Customers From Hell.

2. Ask participants to form small groups of three or four people. One person in each group will be the dealer while the others will be the players. Have each group pick the dealer.

3. Distribute one deck of difficult customer cards to the dealer—Part A of Activity 90. Distribute one copy of the blank answer sheet (Part B) to all the remaining participants. Participants may also use the definitions from Activity 89 to assist them with identifying the different Customers From Hell. Make sure everyone has a pen or pencil with which to record the answers.

4. Explain the rules as follows. Each dealer goes through the deck as quickly as possible; s/he holds up a card with a quote on it, then the other players indicate on the answer sheet whether the quote is from a customer going *through* hell (CGTH) or a Customer From Hell (CFH), and identify which of the Customers From Hell it is. The person with the most right answers is the winner. (Note: Prizes are optional.)

5. When all the cards have been held up, the group members may debate their answers among themselves.

6. Reassemble the entire group and have everyone compare notes on their choice of customer type. Answers are in Part C.

PART A
Game Card Pack

Copy as many pages as needed and cut into individual cards.

✂

"Can you help me? The last person I spoke to had no clue what to do."	"Honestly, if you don't call the manager right this minute, I'm going to start telling everyone in here that this place is a rip-off. Then I'll call John, the owner."

This activity is available at: www.amacombooks.org/go/101ActDKYSOS
© 2009 AMACOM, a division of American Management Association.

"That's just not good enough. I want it replaced and that's all I'll accept."

"Hey look, I really think this is lousy. These directions don't help at all."

"Every time I shop here I have a problem of some sort. What kind of business are you running?"

"This $%^**& place should be out of business. All of you are stupid idiots. I am so !#c$i*& tired of the lousy help here, I could scream."

"Here is the complete file on this product and the problems I have had. I insist that you do exactly what I tell you now, or I'm going to assume someone is out to get me."

It's my lucky day. I get to talk to customer service yet again. I'm so special."

"Don't tell me to calm down. I haven't had such bad service since I left the war. You can talk to me like an adult."

"I really need to talk to Anthony. He's the one who has helped me in the past. He knows my situation better than anyone else."

PART B
Answer Sheet

Does the quote represent a customer going through hell (CGTH) or a Customer From Hell (CFH)?

1. _____   6. _____

2. _____   7. _____

3. _____   8. _____

4. _____   9. _____

5. _____   10. _____

PART C
Answers

1. "Can you help me?"
   CTH—Blasé Blue

2. "Honestly, if you don't call the manager…"
   CFH—Egocentric Edgar

3. "That's just not good enough."
   CFH—Freeloading Freda

4. "Hey look, I really think…"
   CTH—Ornery Orange

5. "Every time I shop here…"
   CTH—Ornery Orange or Raging Red

6. "This $%^**& place…"
   CFH—Bad-mouth Betty

7. "Here is the complete file on this…"
   CFH—Dictatorial Dick

8. "It's my lucky day."
   CTH—Blasé Blue

9. "Don't tell me to calm down…"
   CTH—Hysterical Harold

10. "I really need to talk to…"
    CTH—Ornery Orange

ACTIVITY 91

A Question of Control

Service providers need to find ways to give customers the sense of security that comes from working with knowledgeable professionals, without undermining or threatening the customer's decisional prerogatives. In other words, we have to leave intact the customer's sense of control over the situation. Remember, first "fix" the customer, then fix the problem.

PURPOSE:

✓ To script flexible responses to recurring tough customer situations

✓ To practice skills for fixing both the customer and the problem

TIME: 20 minutes (Consider combining with Activity 77 and/or Activity 86.)

DIRECTIONS:

1. Distribute copies of Part A of Activity 91 and have everyone read the sample situations with an eye toward making recommendations for handling their own typical tough situations. Suggested responses are provided as models for the next part of the activity.

2. Discuss some typical difficult situations in your service organization. Draw up a list of them on a chart pad or white board.

3. Have the participants form small groups of two to four people each. The groups will select one of the situations to develop a script for handling difficult situations. Distribute copies of Part B so they can write their scripts. Allow 7–9 minutes.

4. Reassemble the large group and have the teams read their scripts. Use the following questions for discussion:

    •   What is your comfort level using the scripts that have been written?

    •   What is your anticipation of customer reaction to the scripted comments?

    •   Where do you think there will be problems or challenges?

5. Collect the scripts and ask a volunteer to write them up for distribution to each participant. Challenge them to use them and report their experience at a future meeting.

PART A

Situation 1

•   CUSTOMER: "I need to know who to call for that information. Who do I have to call?"

•   SERVICE PROVIDER: "It is frustrating when you aren't sure who can help. I'd like to try to help you. Please tell me what you need. If I can't help, I'll find the right person, and stay on the line until the transfer goes through. Alright?"

Situation 2

•   CUSTOMER: "Quite frankly, I don't care what your policy is. I want this fixed and fixed now!"

•   SERVICE PROVIDER: "It's clear to me that you are frustrated because your situation is outside the bounds of my authority. Let me tell you what your options are and you can tell me how you would like to proceed. I do want to make this right for you and if we work together, I'm sure we can make that happen."

PART B

1. Description of my "tough customer" situation.

    _____

    _____

    _____

    _____

    _____

    _____

    _____

    _____

2. My suggested response to fix the person and fix the problem.

    _____

    _____

    _____

    _____

    _____

    _____

    _____

SECTION FIVE

Knock Your Socks Off Fitness

Customer service professionals have some of the most challenging jobs that exist. While they don't face the physical demands of operating a jackhammer under a searing sun, or moving a piano to a third-floor walk-up apartment, the emotional labor in dealing with customers all day, day in and out—while also meeting efficiency or productivity goals—can test even the most people-friendly, upbeat, and resilient among us. And we don't need to tell you how stress levels can ratchet up when you're facing Customers From Hell.

This situation makes it all the more vital that your staff not overlook its own emotional health while handling the business of taking care of customers. Long shifts of people contact and problem solving can be invigorating and rewarding, but they also can take their toll if service workers don't monitor their physical and emotional states. Finding ways to release pent-up stress off stage, ensuring that long stretches of keyboard, headset, or computer screen use don't lead to rigor mortis, and developing coping strategies for dealing with customers who get personal are imperative techniques for maintaining one's well-being.

You are no good to anyone—not yourself, your customers, your workmates, or your family—when you're feeling burned out, negative, thorny, or just plain running on fumes. Stress is a reality of life, but how we manage it makes all the difference in how we live up to our promises to deliver consistent *Knock Your Socks Off Service* to external and internal customers. Service "fitness" also means ensuring that your repertoire of service skills includes variety and is up to date. By continually honing your computer skills, refreshing your knowledge of the company's products and services, and sharpening your interpersonal acumen, you equip yourself with the toolkit necessary to keep your service at a world-class, Knock Your Socks Off level.

The activities in this section will help your staff calm their minds, find constructive ways to relieve their stress, stay positive on the job, be continuous learners, and also find time to celebrate their co-workers—and themselves—for the great service they provide to customers.

ACTIVITY **92**

Stress Reducers

Service providers aren't good to anyone when they're stressed up, stressed out, overwrought, anxious, moody, belligerent, nasty—and still waiting for that first cup of coffee. The emotional energy needed in modern service jobs can be more draining than the physical energy needed to lift boxes or pour concrete.

PURPOSE:

✓ To make service providers aware of the importance of managing stress

✓ To familiarize service providers with simple ways to reduce stress

TIME: 20 minutes

DIRECTIONS:

1. Distribute copies of Part A of Activity 92, and review with participants the 10 stress reducers.

2. Distribute copies of Part B and have participants read the brief scenarios, then match the appropriate stress reducers to each scenario. (Note: There may be more than one stress reducer that is applicable to a situation.)

3. Divide the group into smaller groups of three to four people each. Have the groups each create two of their own scenarios and determine the most appropriate reducers for those situations. Allow 5 to 7 minutes for their work.

4. Reassemble the entire group and ask participants to report on their scenarios and what stress reducer they suggested.

5. Discuss with the participants what they have learned in this activity and gather their input for how best to cope with the stress in their jobs. Build a collective plan for the work group.

PART A

10 Stress Reducers

1. *Breathe*. Deep breathing is one of the oldest and best stress-busting techniques. Stress can upset the normal balance of oxygen and carbon dioxide in your lungs. Deep breathing corrects this imbalance and can help you control panic thinking at the same time.

2. *Smile*. You make your mood, and your mood can stress or relax you. Smiling is contagious. When you see a customer looking a little glum, make eye contact and turn on one of your best and brightest. Ninety-nine times out of a hundred, you'll get a smile right back.

3. *Laugh*. Maintaining a sense of humor is your best defense against stress. Stress psychologist Frances Meritt Stern tells of a difficult client she had been dealing with for years. "That clown is driving me up a wall!" she often complained. One day, she began to envision him clownlike, with a white face, floppy shoes, and a wide, foolish grin. With this picture tickling her funny bone, she was able to manage her stress response and focus on doing her job.

4. *Let it out*. Keep your anger and frustration locked up inside, and you are sure to show it on the outside. Instead, make an appointment with yourself for later to think about a particularly stressful customer and then find a way to release the frustration in a private setting.

5. *Take a one-minute vacation*. John Rondell, a sales consultant, creates a vivid mental image of himself snorkeling off a beautiful white-sand beach in the Caribbean. He has worked on the scene until he can transport himself there and lose all sense of time and place, even though his visits last only a minute or two. He often goes to his "favorite place" following a stressful call or before talking to a stress-inducing customer.

6. *Relax.* We tend to hold in tension by tightening our muscles. Instead, try isometrics, tensing and relaxing specific muscles or muscle groups. Make a fist, then relax it. Tighten your stomach muscles, then relax them. Push your palms against each other, then relax your arms. Some people get so good at this they can do their exercises right under the customer's nose.

7. *Do desk aerobics.* Exercise is a vital component of a stress-managed life. Try these two "desk-er-cizes":

   • While sitting at your desk, raise your feet until your legs are almost parallel to the floor. Hold them there for three seconds, then let them down. Do this five times.

   • Rotate your head forward and from side to side (but not back—that can strain rather than stretch). Roll your shoulders forward and then lift them up and back. This feels especially good after you've been sitting or standing for some time.

8. *Organize.* Being organized gives you a sense of control and lessens your stress. "I organize the top of my desk whenever I am waiting on hold," says Eric Johnson, a telephone customer service representative. "Before I leave for the day, I make sure everything is put away, and that I have a list of priorities made out for the next day."

9. *Talk positive.* Vent your anger and frustration in positive ways. Sharing customer encounters with co-workers helps you find the humor in the situation and gain new ideas for handling similar situations. But constant negative talk that rehashes old ground will only re-create and reinforce, not diminish, your stress.

10. *Take a health break.* Change your normal breaks into stress breaks. Consider walking outside, reading a chapter from a favorite book, or just sitting with your eyes closed for a few minutes. Bring healthy snacks and juice to work to substitute for the standard coffee and candy bars.

PART B

Read the situations on the next page on the left column and choose the best stress reducer from the right. Note that there may be more than one right answer, based on individual needs.

Stressful Situation	Stress Reducer
1. "I'm so tired today and I have so much to do. How am I going to get it all done without pulling my hair out and taking it out on my customers?"	1. Breathe
	2. Smile
	3. Laugh
2. "Hi, Mrs. Gomez. Thanks for holding. I'm sorry, I'm still unable to find the information you need. I realize you need it right away, but there's no one in the office who has access to what you need right now."	4. Let it out
	5. Take a one-minute vacation
	6. Relax
	7. Desk aerobics
	8. Organize
	9. Talk positive
	10. Take a health break
3. "Argh! My bus was late, it's pouring rain, my shoes don't match, and I'm late for my performance review!"	
4. "Of course, Rachel… I'll be happy to cover for you again. Why would today be any different from the last three weeks?"	
5. "Where is that report? It was here yesterday and now it's nowhere to be found. Okay, who's been in my cubicle and who took my report?"	
6. "I can't believe it's 3:30 already. I don't think I've left my desk all day and now I've got to meet with Mr. Chi and he's always so demanding."	
7. "I'm terribly sorry, Mrs. Lampa, my computer just froze up again. And I'm afraid I lost the details of your order. Would you be kind enough to start over from the beginning one more time? What was your address again?"	
8. "She just wouldn't stop! She just pointed her finger right in my face and kept yelling and swearing and calling me an idiot. Doesn't she know I didn't do it on purpose?"	

This activity is available at: www.amacombooks.org/go/101ActDKYSOS
© 2009 AMACOM, a division of American Management Association.

ACTIVITY **93**

Create a Stress Log

We all have hot buttons that trigger our stress responses, but we're not always fully aware of what those buttons are. By monitoring the things that set us off in our service jobs, we become more aware of these hot buttons and better manage our responses in stressful moments.

PURPOSE:

✓ To identify potential hot buttons

✓ To learn ways to diffuse stress

✓ To release pent-up stress by writing down details of difficult episodes

✓ To take steps to change potential outcomes

TIME: 5-minute meeting, followed by a 15-minute meeting the following week

DIRECTIONS:

1. Talk to participants about stress, if necessary, review the Stress Reducers given in Activity 92.

2. Distribute copies of the Stress Log (Activity 93) that follows and have participants maintain the log for the next week. Throughout the day, they should pay attention to times when they have felt stressed, and they should record the details of what caused the stress and their response.

3. Bring the group back together the following week and use the following questions to get participants to discuss the activity.

- What did you learn by tracking your stress triggers and responses for one week?
- What is an example of when you handled a stressful situation well?
- What will you do differently in the future?

This activity is available at: www.amacombooks.org/go/101ActDKYSOS
© 2009 AMACOM, a division of American Management Association.

Stress Log				
Date	**Stress Event**	**My Response**	**What I Learned**	**How I Would Respond Next Time**
Example 2/1	Very busy evening at restaurant. Customer said I brought the wrong order.	Became defensive. Told customer that I brought exactly what he ordered. Offered to bring him something different.	Don't argue with customer. Give customer benefit of doubt in cases like this.	Apologize for the misunderstanding and bring a new order as quickly as possible.

ACTIVITY **94**

Coping with Change

Dealing with change in a fast-paced service environment can be a real challenge. Change is a constant for businesses these days: economic ups and downs, changing demands of customers, new technologies, challenges of doing more with less. Trying to keep up with everyday work demands and adapting to change can be a tough double whammy.

PURPOSE:

✓ To support associates dealing with change

✓ To encourage productive behaviors that help move people forward and discourage clinging to the past

✓ To open up conversation about the stresses that change creates

TIME: 30 minutes

DIRECTIONS:

1. Explain to participants that this activity is designed to acknowledge the stresses of dealing with change in a fast-paced environment.

2. Ask participants to describe the ways things are changing in their environment. Record these changes on chart paper or white board for everyone to see.

3. Ask the participants to form small groups of three to four people each. Distribute copies of Part A of Activity 94 and have them respond as teams to form their lists. Allow 4 to 6 minutes for this task.

4. Reassemble the entire group so the teams can present the lists they have created. Record these suggestions on chart paper or white board so everyone can see the lists.

5. Ask the group to study the list of behaviors that help people move ahead. Have them pick their top three behaviors—those that will help the most and have the greatest positive impact. Allow just a minute or two for them to record their choices where indicated on the bottom of Part A.

6. Tally the votes and mark with a check (✓) those behaviors on the master list. Identify the top four behaviors by highest vote count.

7. Assign each small group one of these behaviors and ask the groups to complete Part B. (Note: If there are a small number of people, either form pairs or select only the top three behaviors for further work.) Allow 7 or 8 minutes for this work.

8. Have the whole group assemble again and ask the teams to present their recommendations. Open up the discussion on how to reinforce these behaviors by using the following questions:

   • How will these behaviors help us all deal with change in a better, more positive way?

   • What will it take for each of us to commit to demonstrate these behaviors?

   • What consequences should there be if someone doesn't demonstrate these behaviors?

9. Ask for a volunteer to collect the papers, record all the recommendations, and distribute them to the group.

PART A

In your small group, generate a list of individual attitudes, traits, and characteristics that would be perceived as (1) holding a group back from progress toward defined changes; or (2) moving a group forward toward defined changes. Record the responses on the form.

Behaviors That Inhibit or Encourage Change

Holding Back	Moving Ahead
Example Complaining to your co-worker	Finding something positive in the change

List the most critical behaviors to help individuals or groups cope with change:

_____

_____

_____

_____

PART B

1. Your group has been assigned the behavior:_____ .

2. Determine in your group some specific ways to demonstrate this behavior in the work environment. Think about this from the perspective: "If I were to consider you more _____, what would that look like?"

   a. What would you be saying?

      _____

      _____

      _____

   b. What would you be doing?

      _____

      _____

      _____

ACTIVITY 95

The Web of Support

When you're dealing with change, it's important to have a web or network of people who can offer support. Service jobs have built-in stress, and that stress is magnified in periods of significant change. Developing a network of diverse supporters and confidants can help service providers through these tough times.

PURPOSE:

✓ To assist participants in creating or identifying their own support networks

✓ To analyze the support characteristics and skills offered by work associates

TIME: 20 minutes

DIRECTIONS:

1. Explain to participants that the goal of this activity is to support them in a changing environment. This is a personal and individual activity.

2. Distribute copies of Part A of Activity 95. Review the different types of supporters they may have.

3. Distribute copies of Part B and ask participants to spend some time individually filling in the form. Allow 8 to 10 minutes.

4. Reassemble the group and use the following questions to have a short discussion:

    • What did you learn about your support network from this analysis?

- How many of you have a hole in your web of supporters?
- Who has someone in the work environment who might be supportive of you?
- Don't answer out loud, but how does that person support you in the change we are going through?
- What might you be able to do to round out your support network?

5. Distribute copies of Part C and review the tips with the group.

PART A

Types of Supporters

- *Emotional comforters.* These are caring listeners who allow you to voice your feelings without judging you. They offer support, empathy, and understanding: "Oh, I can see why you'd be anxious."

- *Emotional clarifiers.* These are active listeners who help you sort out and name the feelings you are experiencing: "You seem really sad." "You say you aren't angry yet your fists are clenched."

- *Rational clarifiers.* These provide information and/or perspective to move you beyond your present point: "From my experience, there are two additional skills needed to succeed there."

- *Rational challengers.* These cause us to reconsider our feelings, with questions like "Is that fact or opinion?" and "What would you gain from that?" or statements like, "That doesn't seem reasonable to me."

- *Conformers.* These are opinionated people who are less concerned with helping you sort out your thoughts and feelings than with telling you their ideas: "You shouldn't feel that way."

This activity is available at: www.amacombooks.org/go/101ActDKYSOS
© 2009 AMACOM, a division of American Management Association.

PART **B**
Access Your Network

1. Identify the friends, family, co-workers, professionals, and organizations you view as current or potential resources for support during a change.

   _____

   _____

   _____

2. Identify the type of support (Part A) each person or organization provides and write names or initials in the appropriate space(s) below.

Emotional Reactions	**Rational Reactions**
Comforters (*provide empathy and understanding*)	Clarifiers (*give information and perspective*)
Clarifiers (*identify and interpret feelings*)	Challengers (*challenge thinking, action, or inaction*)

Conformers
(*try to influence your behavior to confirm with their ideas*)

PART C
Tips for Building Your Web of Support

1. Analyzing your support system will better ensure that you get the kind of support you want. Recognize who has what to offer; you can't ask associates to give something they're incapable of providing. "If you go to the grocery store for nails, you're setting yourself up for disappointment."

2. Support providers are often well intentioned, but untrained. Help them help you by telling them directly what it is you want from your interaction. "I don't want advice; I just want you to listen" will probably get you emotional comfort such as "I'm so sorry that happened to you. You must be very disappointed." However, "I'm wondering if you see alternatives I'm missing" will likely get you rational clarification such as "Have you considered _____ or _____?"

3. A balanced support system will show that you have support available in each of the four areas of Part B. Ideally, you should have more than one person in each box, so you are not expecting one or two people to fill several roles. That might place an unreasonable burden on a few and leave you without support if they are unavailable. Consider others in your network who might be potential support givers to fill any gaps.

4. Everything does not work for everybody. As you get ideas from your supporters, pick and choose the ideas and suggestions that fit you. However, you may want to experiment with new strategies that have worked for others in similar situations.

5. If you find you are unable to get continuing support or if you want stronger support than your network provides, you may want to seek more professional counsel.

6. Rather than, or in conjunction with, seeking outside support, some find it helpful to clarify what is happening and to sort out their feelings by writing. Keeping a journal to record your feelings and thoughts through a critical change is an effective way to "give voice" to your stress or deeper feelings, and to lend some perspective to difficult situations.

ACTIVITY **96**

The Power of Positive Talk

We've all heard—and probably know deep down—that the impact of a negative statement far outweighs the impact of a positive one. In fact, some studies indicate that the ratio is 9:1. In other words, it takes nine positive comments to override the effects of one negative comment. Pretty startling, isn't it?

PURPOSE:

✓ To emphasize the impact of both positive and negative comments and self-talk

✓ To provide visible reinforcement of the benefits of keeping positive

TIME: 5-minute meeting, 5-day record, 15-minute follow-up meeting

DIRECTIONS:

1. Explain to participants the purpose of the activity. Distribute either a 3 × 5 index card to each participant or use the sample handout for Activity 96.

2. If using 3 × 5 cards, have the participants draw a line down the center of their card. On the left side of the card, they should write the heading "positive comments." On the right side of the card, they should write the heading "negative comments." Ask them to monitor their self-talk and comments for the next five days, tally them each day, and then record the totals—positive on the left, negative on the right. Emphasize that participants need only record the numbers of comments, not note the comments themselves. They may choose to make

personal notes of reactions of others, their own shift in thinking, or the difficulty or ease of making more positive comments.

3. Suggest that, at the end of each day as they tally their comments, their goal for the next day should be to increase the number of positive comments and decrease the negatives. They should repeat this each day, steadily increasing the number of positive comments and decreasing the total of negative comments.

4. Reassemble the group at the end of the five days and use the following questions to develop the discussion of this activity:

- How did your comments change during the week? For example, did you have fewer negative comments as the week wore on?

- What awareness did you gain about the way you talk to yourself and others?

- Did people react differently to you at the end of the week compared to the beginning, as you offered more positive talk?

- How will this change in outlook impact you both inside and outside the workplace?

5. OPTIONAL: Have a brief discussion on the impact of negative versus positive comments. If you record calls in your service unit, you might pull up some quotes from the calls by both customers and service providers, making use of them as both positive and negative examples. You might even have participants rewrite the negative comments to hear how differently they would sound when shifted to a positive framework. (As a manager, you also can reframe some of the negative comments you may not be aware you make to your staff. For example, rather than saying, "We're not resolving enough customer calls on first contact. We have to pick it up," reframe it as, "We have improved the number of calls we resolve on first contact, but we still have a ways to go to reach our target. If we continue to work hard and use the capabilities of the new database, I know we can reach our goal.")

Talk Positive Tally Cards

Positive Comments	Negative Comments
Day 1	Day 1
Day 2	Day 2
Day 3	Day 3
Day 4	Day 4
Day 5	Day 5
Total:	**Total:**

Positive Comments	Negative Comments
Day 1	Day 1
Day 2	Day 2
Day 3	Day 3
Day 4	Day 4
Day 5	Day 5
Total:	**Total:**

ACTIVITY **97**

Keep It Professional

Today, it's common to hear managers proclaim, "Customers are our best friends." But *Knock Your Socks Off Service* professionals know that, for all the light banter and personal fanfare, there's a critical difference between being friendly and having a friendship. What's important, however, is to keep all interactions professional.

PURPOSE:

✓ To learn to stay professional when dealing with friends as customers

✓ To practice putting the customer first

✓ To recognize the importance of professional behavior

TIME: 30 minutes

DIRECTIONS:

1. Ask participants to describe what makes a friendship special. Look for responses like, "It goes beyond the workplace," "It involves personal commitment," "It may take liberties that you can't at work," "You can be crabby with friends," "Friends often use code words or inside jokes."

2. Now, ask participants how they define a friendly customer interaction. Look for responses like, "It's not as close as a friendship," "Courteous," "Helpful," "Objective, honest," "Upbeat; focused on the customer."

3. Distribute copies of Activity 97 and explain that you are giving them a few scenarios of customer interactions. You want them to form small groups and as teams consider if these scenarios are appropriate for a friendly customer interaction. Allow 7 to 8 minutes.

4. Reassemble the group and ask them how they assessed the interactions. Disagreement may be common.

5. Use the following questions to develop the discussion:
    *   What is the chief difference between a relationship with a friend and a relationship with a customer?
    *   What are some of the dangers of getting too "friendly" with customers?
    *   How might customers react if they perceive that you're being too informal with them? What about if you're overly formal?

SCENARIO 1

Tasha is working at the restaurant counter for her shift. A group of her friends arrive, laughing and obviously having a great time. When they see Tasha, they yell and approach her. All the restaurant diners are now looking. Tasha smiles enthusiastically, warmly greets her friends, and asks how their evening is going. She then makes eye contact with her next customers and asks them what she might get for them.

Professional or unprofessional? _____

_____

_____

SCENARIO 2

Sean is working at a big-box retail store. It's a very slow day. He walks behind a display and pulls out his cellphone. As he dials, he peeks around to see if any customers are about. He is absorbed in his call when he is surprised as a customer comes around the display. The customer nods and keeps walking. He asks his friend to hold on and approaches the customer to see if he can help. The customer responds with, "Just looking, thanks." Sean continues his call.

Professional or unprofessional? _____

_____

_____

SCENARIO 3

Andy and Brandon are taking a quick break after a difficult period of nonstop phone calls in the call center. The queue was full for about 75 minutes. They answered questions, solved problems, calmed customer frustrations, and transferred calls to the correct departments. It is a well-deserved break. Sarah, a colleague from another department, approaches them. She enters the conversation, which stays light and clearly is not focused on work. When Sarah tries to ask the question she needs to ask, the men ignore her question and continue the conversation. She again asks her question, this time to one of them directly. They continue their conversation. When Sarah sternly asks once more, the two indicate that they have to get back on the phones, and suggest that Sarah ask someone else in the department.

Professional or unprofessional? _____

_____

_____

Learning Assessment

Learning on the job doesn't cease when you turn in your "Trainee" tag. Like professional athletes, the best customer service people are always in training, always looking for ways to improve performance, always seeking ways to hone their service edge. As with any well-rounded education, your service "fitness" regimen should cover several interrelated areas. There are five basics: technical skills, interpersonal skills, product and service knowledge, customer knowledge, and personal skills. All are critical to success.

PURPOSE

✓ To identify the five basic areas that keep the focus on continual improvement

✓ To raise awareness of the importance of constant learning while on—and even off—the job

TIME: 20 minutes

DIRECTIONS:

1. Distribute copies of Activity 98 and explain that this assessment is a way to test participants' strengths and weaknesses in five core areas. Remind participants that answers are kept confidential, so honesty is encouraged.

2. Allow 15 minutes for them to complete the assessment, including an opportunity to identify areas of strength and areas in which more skill development might be needed.

3. Suggest that participants take the assessment again in 3 months to see if they sense any changes. What improvement has been made in weaker areas?

4. Suggest that participants also get an objective opinion of their strengths and weaknesses from someone else in the work group. In fact, they may ask someone else to complete the assessment of their skills and then compare the responses. This can be a great way to build rapport with an immediate supervisor, as long as the assessment is done in the spirit of continuous improvement and not used in a punitive manner.

5. Encourage participants to ask their supervisor to assist in building a personal and professional development plan to address the areas where skill development is needed.

Individual Learning Assessment

Technical/Systems Skills

1. I have the skills and training to use our telephone and communications technology. ❏ YES ❏ NO

2. I have the skills and training to use my technology in my work. ❏ YES ❏ NO

3. I know how to use organization systems and procedures to serve my customers. ❏ YES ❏ NO

4. When I need assistance using our technology or systems, I seek it in a timely manner. ❏ YES ❏ NO

5. I understand and can complete the paperwork required from my customers, and from me. ❏ YES ❏ NO

Areas of strength: _____

_____

Areas of weakness: _____

_____

Interpersonal Skills

1. I know the behaviors and attitudes that lead customers to say, *"You really knocked my socks off!"*   ❏ YES   ❏ NO

2. I use specific techniques to diffuse angry or frustrated customers.   ❏ YES   ❏ NO

3. I empathize with my customer's perspective.   ❏ YES   ❏ NO

4. I have insight into my own style and how best to respond to the styles of others.   ❏ YES   ❏ NO

5. I develop a feeling of partnership with customers and co-workers.   ❏ YES   ❏ NO

Areas of strength: _____

_____

Areas of weakness: _____

_____

Product and Service Knowledge

1. I can explain how my area's products and services contribute to my organization's overall success.   ❏ YES   ❏ NO

2. I can compare our products and services with those offered by our competitors.   ❏ YES   ❏ NO

3. I have the information I need about new or planned product and service offerings.   ❏ YES   ❏ NO

4. I know the technical terms and jargon, but I can explain in "plain English."   ❏ YES   ❏ NO

5. I know the most frequently asked questions,   ❏ YES ❏ NO
and the answers.

Areas of strength: _____

_____

Areas of weakness: _____

_____

Customer Knowledge

1. I know what customers complain about,   ❏ YES ❏ NO
and what customers compliment us on.

2. I know why customers choose us over our   ❏ YES ❏ NO
competition.

3. I know the "profiles" of my five most important   ❏ YES ❏ NO
customers/customer groups.

4. I know how the service I provide impacts the   ❏ YES ❏ NO
way customers rate us on quality measures.

5. I continually look for new ways to provide   ❏ YES ❏ NO
Knock Your Socks Off Service.

Areas of strength: _____

_____

Areas of weakness: _____

_____

Personal Skills

1. I deal constructively with on-the-job stress.   ❏ YES   ❏ NO

2. I find new challenges and insights, even when   ❏ YES   ❏ NO
    doing "the same old thing" for customers.

3. I organize and prioritize so I get the right things   ❏ YES   ❏ NO
    done, in the right order.

4. When faced with customer frustration or anger,   ❏ YES   ❏ NO
    I don't take it personally.

5. The work I am doing now provides an important   ❏ YES   ❏ NO
    step toward my long-term goals.

Areas of strength: _____

_____

Areas of weakness: _____

_____

ACTIVITY **99**

The Power of Curiosity

Ever wonder about the new theater production that just opened and is getting rave reviews? Or how about that new exhibit at the museum? Want to learn a new software program or Latin dancing? A curious mind keeps us young and invigorated. As you keep learning, you see things from different perspectives, hone your problem-solving skills, and keep an open mind for new ideas.

PURPOSE:

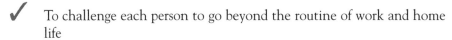 To challenge each person to go beyond the routine of work and home life

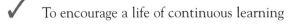 To encourage a life of continuous learning

TIME: Varies

DIRECTIONS:

1. Ask participants to think about people they know who seem interesting and well educated. Ask what these people do to be so interesting and well educated.

2. Explain that the concept of learning and having curiosity challenges participants to try new things. In the next month, each person is encouraged to do something he or she has never done before. Consider the following suggestions for your participants:
   - If they typically go out to dinner once a month, they should try a new restaurant.
   - If they typically go to movies, they might want to try live theater instead.

- If they exercise, they might do a different type of exercise, like biking instead of jogging.
- If they walk regularly, suggest going to a nature preserve or arboretum to walk instead of in the neighborhood.
- If they like to cook, they could invite friends for dinner and serve a new type of food, say Indian, Thai, or vegetarian.
- If they read a certain type of book or magazine, switch to a new genre.
- If they want to learn something new, sign up for a community education class, dance class, or hobby club.

3. Ask participants what new adventure they are willing to try or look into. Get the discussion going about available options.

4. If you have the luxury, offer participants a small amount of money that could be applied to their new adventure. If this option is chosen, require that they report to the group on what, when, and how they used the money.

5. Over the next month, gather comments or responses that participants have tried or done to report back to the whole group as a summary. Even more effective is to have participants talk about their experience soon after it happens to reinforce their willingness to try something new.

For All You Do, This Note's For You

Some people seem born knowing how to give themselves the needed pats on the back for work well done. But for most of us, celebrating ourselves doesn't come easy. That's an attitude that *Knock Your Socks Off Service* professionals can—and should—learn to leave behind. Give yourself permission to be terrific!

PURPOSE:

✓ To celebrate our own service accomplishments

✓ To remind ourselves that we work really hard

✓ To practice saying "thank you" to ourselves

TIME: 10 minutes

DIRECTIONS:

1. When work is particularly stressful, or you have been a fantastic fixer, or you have successfully navigated the waters with an extremely difficult customer, it's time to say thank you for a job well done. Have participants identify specific times when they made an interaction successful.

2. Distribute copies of the activity and have participants write themselves a similar thank-you note, with specific details of the skills they used or work they did. Participants can use either the formatted sample or create one of their own.

3. Collect the thank-you notes and send them through interoffice mail so that the participants receive them later in the day or the next day.

4. Suggest to participants that if it's appropriate, they can give or send a copy of their thank-you note to their immediate supervisor. When doing this, though, they should be specific about the skills they used, problems they solved, or the customer feedback they received to show their success.

5. OPTIONAL: Use this same activity to honor a colleague, practice giving positive feedback, or celebrate successes in your workplace. Bring participants together again and explain the purpose of this additional exercise. Ask that they take the next week looking for ways that their colleagues do a great job with customers. When they see this happen, they are to make note of what specifically was done well. Then, you can distribute additional copies of the sample thank-yous and explain that they may use them or create their own to thank their colleagues.

6. At the next department meeting, ask participants how it made them feel to be recognized by their peers.

Dear _____

Congratulations on a job well done! You demonstrated the following skills in working through this difficult situation:

a. _____

    _____

b. _____

    _____

c. _____

    _____

The customer demonstrated appreciation by saying or doing _____

_____

Keep up the good work!

Dear _____

Congratulations on a job well done! You demonstrated the following skills in working through this difficult situation:

a. _____

_____

b. _____

_____

c. _____

_____

The customer demonstrated appreciation by saying or doing _____

_____

Keep up the good work!

This activity is available at: www.amacombooks.org/go/101ActDKYSOS
© 2009 AMACOM, a division of American Management Association.

ACTIVITY **101**

What's Important to Me?

What turns your crank? Or rings your chimes? What keeps you coming back to work day after day? Motivation is important in the world of *Knock Your Socks Off Service*. Working with people day in and day out can be a difficult job. It's important to know the things that make you relish going to work each day and keep you going through the tough times.

PURPOSE:

✓ To realize that there are many forms of motivation, reward, and recognition

✓ To determine the primary motivators for each person in your work group

✓ To make the point that money is really only a short-term motivator

TIME: 20 minutes

DIRECTIONS:

1. Explain to participants that we are all unique beings motivated in vastly different ways. Some motivators are internal; some are external. The company can be responsive only to external motivators.

2. Distribute copies of Part A of Activity 101 and ask participants to fill in the first column. Allow 5 minutes.

3. Distribute copies of Part B and direct participants to record in the additional two columns the research findings on both manager and employee rankings, and to compare them to their own rankings.

4. Use the following questions to discuss the outcome:

- What surprised you about your ranking?
- How does your ranking compare to that of the other two columns?
- What might be missing from this list?
- How might this help you better communicate with your immediate supervisor on motivation and reward/recognition?

PART A

Rank the motivators listed in the first column, based on their importance to you as an individual, in the second column, ranging from 1 for the most important to 10 as the least important. Then, consider if there are other motivators important to you that are missing from the list, and add them at the bottom of the page.

What Is Important to Me			
Motivators	Your Ranking	Manager Ranking	Employee Ranking
High Wages			
Job Security			
Promotion in the Company			
Good Working Conditions			
Interesting Work			
Personal Loyalty of Supervisor			
Tactful Discipline			
Full Appreciation of Work Being Done			
Help on Personal Problems			
Feeling of Being in on Things			

This activity is available at: www.amacombooks.org/go/101ActDKYSOS
© 2009 AMACOM, a division of American Management Association.

Add your personal motivations below:

What Is Important to Me

Motivators	Your Ranking	Manager Ranking	Employee Ranking

PART B

Motivator	Manager Ranking	Employee Ranking
High Wages	1	5
Job Security	2	4
Promotion in the Company	3	7
Good Working Conditions	4	9
Interesting Work	5	6
Personal Loyalty of Supervisor	6	8
Tactful Discipline	7	10
Full Appreciation of Work Being Done	8	1
Help on Personal Problems	9	3
Feeling of Being in on Things	10	2

Source: Adapted from research conducted by Susan Herrington, Training Consultant, North Tennessee Private Industry Council in Clarksville, Tennessee, 2002.

CREDITS

ACTIVITY 59

Adapted from *The Xers & The Boomers: From Adversaries to Allies* by Claire Raines and Jim Hunt (Crisp Publications, 2000). Used with permission of the author. All rights reserved.

ACTIVITY 66

Diagrams adapted from "Leading Extraordinary Customer Service," a seminar developed by Performance Research Associates and the American Management Association. Used with permission of Performance Research Associates. All rights reserved.

ACTIVITY 81

Adapted from a *Delivering Knock Your Socks Off Service* training program conducted by Performance Research Associates, Inc., at Select Health in Salt Lake City, Utah. Used with permission of Performance Research Associates, Inc.

ACTIVITY 83

The Sudoku puzzle is from Workshops by Thiagi, Bloomington, Indiana. Used with permission of the author. All rights reserved.

ACTIVITY 89

Customers From Hell is a registered trademark of Performance Research Associates, Minneapolis, MN. All rights reserved.

ACTIVITY 101

Data adapted from research presented in a workshop entitled "The Human Side of Organizational Management" on November 24-25, 1996 by Susan Herrington, Training Consultant, North Tennessee Private Industry Council, Clarksville, Tennessee. A link may be found at http://www.naco.org /cnews/1996/96-12-09/manage.htm

INDEX

ABOUT THE AUTHORS

Ann Thomas brings more than twenty years' experience in consulting and training to each of her clients. Her work focuses on improving service quality, diversity awareness, generational differences, sales, performance management, and professional development.

As senior consultant and lead facilitator with Performance Research Associates since 1999, Ms. Thomas' clients include Atlanta Hartsfield-Jackson International Airport; Depository Trust and Clearing Corporation; Marriott ExecuStay, The Mall of America; Hewitt Mobility Services; Advantage Health Systems; Accenture; Universities of Connecticut, Alabama, Iowa, Kansas, Minnesota, and Texas; National Geospacial Agency; the Securities and Exchange Commission; Turner Broadcasting; Retail Packaging Association; Daimler-Chrysler; Plexent; and many others. Ann is a member of the faculty for the American Management Association. She is a regular presenter for Progressive Business Conferences.

Ann does extensive volunteer work in her community. In her off hours Ann enjoys working in her garden, walking, sailing, and spending time with her family.

Jill Applegate is project manager and client coordinator with Performance Research Associates. She served as right hand to the late Ron Zemke for nearly fifteen years and takes seriously the responsibility of the concepts of *Knock Your Socks Off Service* and the importance of wowing customers.

Ms. Applegate works closely with PRA clients to ensure that our collaborative efforts hit the mark. Her responsiveness, attention to detail, and depth of knowledge allow her to not only talk the talk but also walk the walk.

Jill stays busy volunteering in her church, playing the piano, watching football, and taking frequent trips to Disney World and other theme parks, and is proud of her up-to-date roller-coaster résumé.